The
Voyage

*An invitation to learn principles
of entrepreneurship and leadership*

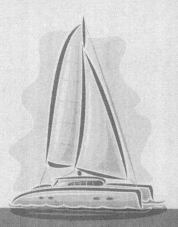

Miguel Aguado Verguizas

The Voyage

*An invitation to learn principles
of entrepreneurship and leadership*

by Miguel Aguado Verguizas

ISBN: 978-1-64142-020-4

Published by

Editorial RENUEVO LLC.
www.EditorialRenuevo.com
info@EditorialRenuevo.com

Contents

I dedicate this book to my dear wife
Pilar, for so much love and wisdom that
she has always given me.

To my children Miguel, Daniel and
Rafael, because they gave meaning to
my life.

To my grandchildren, Monica, Daniel,
Jorge, Ariana and Alex, because they
light up my spirit with the joy of
their smiles.

Prologue

To listen to Miguel in his lectures is to be in the presence of a navigator of life. Throughout the countless nautical, aerial and terrestrial miles that he has traveled and accumulated all over the world—and by saying all over the world, I say it literally—he has also gathered wonderful stories, anecdotes and experiences. One more of his many adventures is the voyage he made across the Atlantic Ocean on a sailboat.

In this book, we have the opportunity to get to know many of those stories and especially the journey that he and a few other friends made from Gran Canaria in Spanish territory, to the Island of Martinique in the American Caribbean. The interesting thing was to have done it on a sailboat, driven by the force of the wind.

Throughout his book, we enjoy a delicious mix of the narrative of that crossing, relevant fragments of his life and, above all, great teachings that invite us to leave our comfort zone to look for new ports and destinations. If his trip across the ocean seems like a great challenge, reading his book is like entering our own ship, because throughout the reading, we discover and receive—challenge after challenge—what Miguel presents to us.

His narrative is simple, fast and entertaining, thanks to its structure based on the navigational log of his maritime adventure. In each chapter, he gives us a perspective of what he was recording day by day on the trip. With this, he invites us to be part of the crew to make us feel what he and the rest of the sailors experienced.

His desire to help us grow and set new goals is reflected on each page, but he also tells us what to do and how to achieve it. His work is a constant invitation for us to become, like him, daring sailors in our own lives.

Thus, in each chapter, in addition to showing us fragments of the logbook, he takes us to moments of his past to understand and get to know the emergence of his adventurous spirit. Day after nautical day we get to know his roots, his challenges and his achievements. A hallmark of his work is that each of his anecdotes becomes a specific and very useful teaching; therefore, there is not a single chapter in which we do not receive teachings and practical ideas to take our lives to the next level, or perhaps I should say, to the next port.

The Voyage is a mixture of adventure, autobiographical data and very valuable self-help material.

I warn readers that they are about to enter this logbook of learning and that as they go through it they will be living the possibility of developing great changes in their lives. In addition to enjoying the descriptions of the sea and its wonders, they will not withstand Miguel's constant invitations to lead our lives, as he rightly says, out to sea.

Rafael Ayala

I remember once when, as a child—I think I was not yet 10 years old—I was in the center of a circle that my friends had formed. It was a kind of game and I had voluntarily put myself in that place. My friends made me go round and round, and if at some point I moved slightly away from the center or it seemed like I was going to fall, they held me up and kept me spinning like a top. Surely the number of laps was less than what I thought, because for a few moments I felt overwhelmed, since the game seemed to have no end. When I finally stopped and they no longer supported me, not only did I feel dizzy, but for a few moments I completely lost my sense of direction.

This situation was repeated when I was 22 years old. No, there were no friends or circle, but a metaphorical dizziness and a lot of disorientation. Without being aware of it, I was having my first existential crisis. The set of beliefs that previously formed the shell that represented my previous mental state, now detached to give way to a breakthrough, my birth into maturity. However, between the comfort of the old and the fear of the new, is the turbulence of the transition. Unlike the game of the circle, it was not a physical dizziness, but like when I was in it, I did not know how to find my north. Would I reach terra firma? Of course, but only after overcoming what Miguel Aguado would call "my surging waves."

These wave surges represented one of the questions that we all have to face at some point: What is the purpose of life? And finding the answer is nothing less than finding the set of values worth living for.

And how to find that solution?

The answer is: through personal experience. However, that experience need not be solitary and the search for solutions may be shortened when the experience is matched with knowledge. That's where the true value of the work you have in your hands comes in.

In this book, Miguel Aguado masterly weaves a whole braid of parallels between the ocean and life, whose purpose is to shed light on the components of our existence that contain the greatest value and their pearls of wisdom.... You will be surprised! Many of them become a paradox, because they are the areas people pay the least attention to even though they have precisely the greatest wisdom.

What is the only thing that differentiates a sailor who manages to cross oceans several times from one who will never do it? The same thing that differentiates an excellent chef from a mediocre one or a successful entrepreneur from one who has not succeeded. Everything is always reduced to one word. That word is: **knowledge**. They know how to do it because they know the way and the keys that lead to what each one calls their own success. The slow way is by investing many years of experience. The fast way is learning from those who have invested them for you. Thank you, dear Miguel.

If this book had existed and had fallen into my hands when I had to pass my first existential surge of waves, perhaps I might not have avoided the gale, but it would have shortened its duration. When you are lost and you spin around your own axis as I did in school, each turn gives you 360 degrees of options and therefore, 360 possible directions in which to move forward. The difficult thing is not to take a single path, since to take a path is easy; the difficult thing is to know which of them is the correct one. If someone could give us that information and that knowledge, it could literally be saving our lives.

That valuable information has just come to you in the form of pages, and you will see its enormous power when you put it into practice to discover that you now have a greater empowerment to take the right paths and, above all, to detect and avoid the wrong directions.

Why isn't there more success in our society? Because it suffers from a lack of leaders who are willing to share that knowledge that has allowed them to reach the point of arrival with those who are still at the point of departure. In the world, there are two types of people: those whose greatest happiness is in empowering others, and those whose only interest is in empowering themselves.

If there is a message that Miguel has not stopped giving me since I have known him, it is his faithful commitment to be among the first. He is a born empowering person and as an empowering person he is familiar with a step in the universal ladder that contains the formula of coherence, which says:

The strongest words are not those that become shouts, but those that become actions.

I love men (and women) of action, and Miguel is. This book is.

Sharing your knowledge, far from reducing your wisdom, makes it bigger; just like sharing a candle—far from reducing its flame, increases your light.

Dear reader, I am convinced that, once you have finished reading this work, you will agree with me in determining that it will be accurate, every time we talk about this creation, figuratively (or not), for us to stop calling it a "book" and start calling it for what it is: "Spring of Wisdom," because this is not a book. It is a *treasure*.

I only have one request for you:

Empty your mind and prepare to discover it.

The greater your predisposition to growth, the greater your attraction of abundance.

Anxo Pérez

Introduction

Welcome Sailors

"Friends, we have a problem. Water is entering one of the hulls of the sailboat." Listening to these words when you are in the middle of the Atlantic, thousands of kilometers from any coast, is like a bucket of ice water on your head.

But if something had to be kept cool in those moments, it was just that, the head. The seven sailboat crew members needed to quickly agree, coordinate and work to resolve the situation immediately. There was no time to lose.

Who forced me to be in these conditions? Why do some people look for adventures and others not even think about them? What is the reason why I did not regret crossing the Atlantic on a catamaran[1] for a second? Why take risks? Why dare? Silliness or immaturity? Prolonged youth? A suicidal act? None of the above. The reason arises from that seed that we carry inside and that I call: the seed of the sailor.

The human spirit has the wonderful gift of modifying its present through the decisions it makes. We can spend our lives shut up in brick and metal structures or choose to have the sky, the water and the air be our roof, floor and walls. My spirit, like that of any sailor, has not been willing to sit still and let the circumstances add flavor to my life. No, my days—which in the eyes of others have been many and in mine a breath—I have seasoned with boldness and adventures that I have shared with my wife, children and friends.

After over seven decades, I have reflected on what I have experienced, and now I see, with more satisfaction than longing, that there are constants throughout my journey. These have forged what I am now, and at the time they offered enjoyment and cheer; of course, also sadness, but never despair. This is something that the sea teaches us. Beyond that endless blue carpet there is solid ground to reach, a longed-for destination.

In these pages I wish to tell you, through moments of my life, the story of any sailor; maybe your own story or the one you can start from now on. My purpose is to be

---

1 A catamaran is a boat with two parallel hulls of equal size, joined by a platform. They are driven by the contact of the wind in their sails and usually have an engine.

a gust of wind that propels your sails toward the desired destination. It is possible, it only requires awakening the traveler who perhaps you put to sleep based on custom— that audacious walker who let himself become lethargic when walking the path that most travel. Within us there is that hunger for adventure, nature and knowledge. There is in you and in me, that inclination to challenge, achievement and victory.

Although I was born far from the coast, my heart was formed permeated by the rolling of the waves. *In me there was a seed of salt water.* And although I have lived in friendship with the sea, I am convinced that to embark is more than setting sail on a ship; it is a lifestyle, a way to face challenges and our dreams.

Sailing involves living by choice, not by chance. Daring to enjoy and hanging on to survival. You are a sailor like me. We were not created to subsist, but to conquer ports, to contribute to the world, to develop our talents and to embark on new things. I do not know what seed you have in your heart, but I assure you that you have it. In you there are seeds with enough potential to take you to greater fulfillment, to enjoy, to know yourself better and to unleash the talents you have.

These are not just words to motivate you; they describe a reality. The human being is a wonderful creation. It is not the strongest creature, nor the biggest and not the fastest. There are animals that surpass us by far in all those qualities; nevertheless, man governs the planet by his mind and willpower. This world is the territory of sailors; it is designed for them. Maybe that's why seventy percent of the planet is water. Its outline suggests we go out to sea.

The sailor cannot adapt to boredom, to tasting the simple-minded flavor of a Sunday afternoon and, resigned, wait for the arrival of another Monday. He is an entrepreneur, a man or a woman who sees beyond what his eyes see; they watch with their imagination, the fuel of their dreams sustains them, and they know that behind the horizon there is a region beyond.

Of course, this determined spirit involves risks. There is no entrepreneurship without them. I have lived through them. Leaving the port puts you at the mercy of the ocean, with its rules and principles. But the sea, like life, is a lady; if you respect her, she will do the same to you, even if it involves important challenges; like the one we experienced that night when the water leaked into our catamaran.

This way of life involves launching out to sea and giving up seeing the coast in the hope of finding it several weeks later. Also to face waves seven meters high and realize how small you are; to endure downpours and swells and then to float motionless four kilometers from the bottom of the ocean; to sustain yourself on the water without wind, without waves; stopped in the middle of the huge Atlantic mirror; surrounded only by sky, water and silence.

This is part of what the sailor lives, that human being who

is not satisfied by solid ground, who seeks to embark and discover. His boldness breaks the comfort of the known, the routine of the office and even the land where he was born. All this with the aim of not settling for what has been achieved. He refuses to reproduce what is dictated for the majority: being born, studying, working, earning money and retiring.

The spirit of the navigator unleashes the need to honor our nature in order to reveal the potential that God deposited in us. Yes, sailing implies dangers, but staying on dry land and continuing with the routine is worse. ***Living an unhappy and routine life is not even a greater risk— it is the acceptance of failure.*** It's a defeat with dozens of disguises—masks of success, money, responsibility, security, prestige or victims.

This collection of experiences and teachings will show you how to germinate the seed of the sailor within you.

I invite you to go with me through fragments of my navigation logbook. In it I recorded the sailboat crossing of the entire width of the Atlantic Ocean. From Spain to the Caribbean. In those pages I wrote the technical navigation requirements, as well as the thoughts and reflections I made along the way. I hope my anecdotes and recommendations are the water that makes your seed bloom and the wind that fills your sails.

Welcome aboard!

WE SET SAIL

Nautical Day[2] 1
Crossing: Las Palmas de Gran Canaria to Martinique Island.
E.T.D.[3] 11.10.2016.
E.T.A. 12.1.2016 or 12.2.2016

---

2   Nautical Day is the nautical term to refer to 24 hours, one day. Only it is usually counted from 12 noon.
3   E.T.D. and E.T.A. mean time or estimated time of departure and arrival, respectively, according to their acronyms in English.

The sun was celebrating another autumn day over the port of Las Palmas, on the island of Gran Canaria, a Spanish territory of 1,560 square kilometers off the coast from the Moroccan Sahara Desert. My six companions and I were in *El Impulso*, the twelve by seven meter catamaran in which we were preparing to sail the Atlantic. Our destination—the island of Martinique in the American Caribbean.

After a lot of planning, calculations and conversations with sailors who had made the trip, we calculated that it would take us twenty days to reach America. In the environment, we breathed that mixture of enthusiasm and nervousness which, although you have set out to sea, you do not stop experiencing in the face of a new journey, and with more reason, when it comes to crossing the Atlantic with the force of the wind. These types of tours are those that even a lover of the sea and adventure, performs only once or twice in their life; although many sailors never live it, I'm sure every sailor wants to.

Looking out to sea, ships of all sizes and flags could be seen. The multitude of boats was due to the excellent geographical location of the port, since it is the natural Atlantic route to connect Europe with Africa and the gateway to both continents for boats from America. Despite the bustle that characterizes Las Palmas—yachts entering and leaving the marina, people moving about; large freighters, cranes loading containers and other port activity—my attention and focus were on reviewing all the obligatory details prior to setting sail. Each of the sailors had their responsibilities on the ship; we had discussed and agreed to them earlier and reaffirmed them the previous night.

My encounter with the sea

When making sure that my responsibilities were covered, I began to think why, at seventy-two, I was beginning this adventure. My mind flew to my childhood. I was born in Madrid, which, at that time, like the rest of the country, was still recovering from the civil war that engulfed the country. Austerity and scarcity were still manifest in the houses. My father was a hard worker. Every morning he started the day with the blue gray before dawn, and concluded it when we already had our pajamas on. He worked in various jobs in the government and did everything in his power to be a good provider for the family.

I met my first love, and one that I would keep the rest of my life, when I was around five years of age. In those days, a brother of my father who lived in the north of the country was getting married. My parents, for some reason that I do not know, took me to the wedding with them. The sun was still asleep when we got in the car in Madrid. A good part of the journey I slept in the back of the car, while they talked about their things. From time to time, I enjoyed looking through the window at the green and yellow colors of the crops we were passing on the highway. I remember the smell with a mixture of coffee, firewood and sausages that we breathed where we stopped to eat. It was a small house on the edge of the road, I think near Villacastín. Fried eggs, toast with jam and coffee with milk.

Later, I was surprised to see the reflection of the sun on a large expanse of water surrounded by trees and mountains. It looked like an immense mirror with curved shapes in the middle of the landscape. I asked my father if that was the sea. After laughing a little together with my mother, he explained that no, it was an accumulation of water trapped by a barrier called a reservoir.

"The sea is much bigger; much, much bigger," my mother told me. It was hard for me to imagine more water in one place than what I had just seen.

Hours later, climbing the mountain and riding through the forest, we arrived at the Port of Gijón. It was not the buildings with yellow stone walls and tile roofs that amazed me; nor observing the fish in the Pelayo fountain.

The scene that struck me forever was seeing the sea. I had never imagined such magnitude. It was a water giant! An eternal tablecloth, a liquid miracle that danced all the time. A spectacular landscape: the purity of its color, the sparkling break of the waves and its encounter in the distance, far away, with the sky. What I had seen in the movies was far from what I was witnessing. It could be heard, smelled and breathed.

As if this were not enough, my parents, some uncles and I, took a tour in a small motor boat. Feeling the breeze on my face and understanding that I could sail away on that liquid titan sealed my heart or rather, sowed my seed. That blessed day, on that Asturian beach, I discovered one of the passions that would accompany me all my life.

From that moment, the ocean was tattooed on my mind. Its presence would no longer leave me. I started watching pirate movies and marine adventures; I played by pretending to be sailing the oceans, and every time there was an opportunity to go to a beach, I was the first to raise my hand so they would consider me. I kept my passion strong, just like one bottles up that strange throbbing that a special girl in elementary school produces in you. I imagine that they—or at least my father—could not see the magnitude of the dream that the encounter in Gijón awakened, because many years later, when I told him that I wanted to be a sailor, he was greatly surprised.

The power of a dream

That is the power of a dream. Now, sixty-seven years after

that visit to the port, here I was, once again ready to set sail, ready to embrace my great lady, the sea, again. But now I would not do it on a huge commercial ship, nor on the first ship I bought myself, Freedom 1. No, this time we would **cross the Atlantic by sailing, with the force of the wind, the grace of God and the work and hope of six other dreamers.**

What is your dream? I am sure that within you live longings that you identified since childhood. Maybe you thought that they were only unviable imaginations, follies of youth or childhood; but irresponsibility or nonsense for the adult stage. It is not like this. Dreams are the engine that continues to be latent inside you and you need to relive. A person who doesn't dare to remove the cover that hides his dreams doesn't enjoy work, his mornings and nights, money and his friends. By forgetting those desires, we weaken our sense of enjoyment.

Maybe we attain financial achievements, professional positions or even, we accumulate beautiful and valuable assets; however, nothing satisfies us completely.

The reason is that we were not created to amass riches, have a job or say we have a stable family. No, life, like the sea, is much bigger. Of course, we can have and look for all of the above, but we should not do so at the price of giving up what we were created for. We are sailors, seekers of new opportunities, sailors with passions, longings, hope and dreams.

We have to dig through the memories of our soul until we

find the trunk where those expectations were left. Those dreams that awakened our imagination and excited us completely. I know that inside you they still exist, they keep beating; maybe with little strength, but it's a matter of reviving them. Dare yourself!

Take a notebook and a pen and write down the list of things you want. Make sure they are not goals that you are supposed to want. Dig deep into yourself, uncover your dreams, remove the rubble behind which you have hidden them. What would you like to reach, do, have or achieve before your life ends? What reality will make you feel proud and full? What is the venture that burns in your heart? What idea, when it returns to your mind, inspires you and fills you with energy? **What would you spend your time and resources on, if money was not a problem?**

Stop a few seconds or maybe, much more than that. Return to read the questions I have shared with you and reflect on this. Your answers will uncover your dreams.

Start your odyssey with this first step. Record your wishes and prioritize them. Number each one in order of importance and then share them with the people you love. Announce that inside you there is a sailor eager to travel new latitudes. In doing so, your dreams begin to come alive, they become expression and words produce commitments, detonate actions. Do not pay attention to your age, your current circumstances and money. At this time, just focus on resurrecting your desires.

A trip should always start by establishing the destination. That destiny is to reach your dreams.

"Release the moorings," I heard Enrique shout. I awoke from my reflections and went to the bow. From there, with the help of a man on the shore, we released the ropes, freeing the catamaran from its mooring, and *El Impulso* began to move. The tingling in my belly warned me that the adventure was beginning. This dream went from imagination, writing, words and meetings, to being a reality.

The shore faded away and the view of the port of Las Palmas grew wider, and minutes later, far away and small. **Behind us was the mainland; ahead, only the marine immensity.**

DEFINING
THE DESTINATION

2nd Nautical Day 11.11.2016

We moved along with a strong crosswind, although after the first hours of the day its strength was reduced to about 20 knots. The ship's speed was maintained at an average of 6.5 knots.

Since we set sail, the crew member who had the least experience at sea felt sick. It was the normal seasickness from when you go out to sea. The rocking of the boat in the arms of the waves produces that terrible effect. It is an undesirable feeling that affects your whole body and of course, also your mood.

All of us who have sailed the great seas, have had it happen more than once. And when you experience it, you would pay to be on solid ground. It is a terrible feeling. Also, since you suffer it when the trip is just beginning, you think it won't disappear for the rest of the voyage and you have too many days before it will be over. It is a waking nightmare. Faced with this physical discomfort, the only recourse is to lie down, rest, hydrate and wait for the body to get used to the movement, until you "marinize[4]". That's what we recommended to our friend. But when you're like this, you think the dizziness won't go away, because the boat doesn't stop moving.

Unpleasant situations like this appear to those who go out to sea. It's part of the price of going after your dreams. However, when you have your destiny in your mind, the problems become obstacles to be resolved, not reasons to surrender. Therefore, it is essential to be clear about the end of our journey. All the crew had dreamed of crossing the Atlantic on a sailboat; leaving Spanish soil and taking the ship to a Caribbean port. This was not just another activity of our lives, it was the achievement of a dream.

In the previous nautical day, I invited you to relive your desires, because I know they are fuel for the spirit. Reaching them implies leaving the port. I know that in a marina the boats look beautiful, but they were not created to be parked in a marina, but to sail.

Many people never set sail and lose sight of the coast. They seek to maintain a security that will not give them the happiness they crave. They remain in their routine out of fear or to avoid making decisions. They stay in their comfort zone.

---

4   Popular term among sailors to refer to getting used to the movements of the boat without feeling nauseated.

Without a destination, there is no voyage and without goals, there are no results

When a sailor sets sail, he knows where he is going, he has in mind the place where he will arrive. That is what his navigation map depends on. Whenever he leaves, he does it with a goal. *Without a destination, there is no voyage.* If it were not so, there would be no route to follow, storms to traverse, or crew to recruit. Our life must be the same. We must turn dreams into clear goals, determine our port of arrival. It is useless for the winds to fill the sails of our boat if we do not know where we are going.

I propose then, dear sailor, that you establish your "why" and "what for". Once your dreams are revived, find out what is behind them, why they excite you, what makes them worth facing efforts and risks. What would you achieve if you reached them? What is the impact they will have on your life or the lives of others?

Take time to answer these questions. When you answer them, you will see how your desires get stronger, or if they are not relevant, how they vanish. Once you have identified them, you will be ready to convert them into goals. This step is key to planning specific actions. While your longings are only dreams, they will be just that; but when you polish them and make them goals, then they become more real, more feasible to work on.

Next, I will share several steps to transform your dreams into goals and achieve them.

1. **Make them specific.** This means that you must itemize them instead of writing generalities. For example, instead of saying that you want to travel the world, write down the places you want to visit. If your dream is to have a business of your own, make it specific, writing what kind of business you want it to be. My dream could be to navigate the world, but when I turned it into a goal, I decided to cross the Atlantic on a sailboat leaving Gran Canaria to reach the Island of Martinique.

2. **Turn them into something measurable.** To do this, you must write them in such a way that you can clearly know what progress you have made, and how far or near you are from reaching them. The measurements include quantities and dates. For example, instead of noting that you want to save enough money for your old age, write down a specific amount to collect by a specific date. If your dream is to write a book, write down when you want to see it concluded. If in the case of traveling around the world you wrote down, for example, visiting Brazil and Argentina, record the deadline for doing so. Then, you can affirm that you will go to those countries in the summer of the year that you specified. This will allow you to plan what you must do to achieve it in the time you defined.

3. **Make an itinerary.** Consider the series of steps you must take to reach your goal. *Objectives are not achieved with a single act. They are the place where we arrive after going through a process;*

after performing a series of tasks that, when added together, end in the result. But making a travel route does not only require knowing the destination; it also requires determining where we are. We must recognize what we have and what we need to learn or have. Every plan contains three points: where I am, where I am going and what path to follow. So our voyage required previous investigation, how to get information, get a boat, put together a team and many other things. Your goals also require many actions. Make a list of them, as they will be the source for designing your navigation map that shows the path we are going to take and helps us to measure the approximate time our challenge will take and the amount of resources we will need. In our case, we talked with other sailors who had already crossed the Atlantic; we investigated and read about it and specifically about those who had done the feat in a boat similar to ours. All this helped us determine how many of us would travel, the amount of food and water we would need, the tools that would be advisable to carry, etc. And we had to attend to these and many other activities to set sail with real possibilities of reaching the desired destination.

4. **Respect your values and other people.** *It is important that what you decide to achieve and how you do it is congruent with your beliefs.* Also, you should ensure that no one is harmed in the process. Integrity is the source that gives us peace along the way. It is of little use to reach goals if we do not live in peace. Going through life serene, without fear of being exposed as

cheaters because we haven't done any cheating, is one of the great achievements we can have as people. Let's go after our goals doing things correctly.

5. **Write down your goals.** Record your objectives. Remember to edit them to be specific so as to be able to measure them and set a deadline. Try to bring them with you. Place them in visible places to remember them frequently. Have them on your phone, calendar, the fridge, the bathroom mirror, your car, and so on. It is something that you need to see constantly, because they are the motive that will drive you, they are your fuel. Each activity that arises from the goals, write it down in your appointment book so that you can move forward.

6. **Start right away.** Since you already have a navigation plan, you can start working on the first steps. The work to achieve our goal of crossing the ocean did not begin the day we sailed, but when I had the first conversation about it with Enrique. That was the first step, but then many more followed. As soon as you specify your goals and define where you are relative to them, you can identify small actions to be taken immediately. ***Starting, even with something simple, breaks the inertia that keeps us in the comfort zone.***

7. **Believe firmly that you can achieve your goals.** This is not a technique to produce sidereal magic that does things for you; but it is a fundamental part of taking action. Whoever has doubts about achieving

their goals tries with less strength or, sometimes, never achieves them. People who know that they have the capability to achieve what they propose make decisions about it, move, commit to their dreams and start working toward them. I know you have the potential to achieve your goals; I'm sure of it. I do not have more neurons than you, nor was I born with a special gift. Human beings were created to succeed, to be navigators, to undertake. While we continue breathing we can achieve it.

Crossing the Atlantic on a sailboat was a fantasy I dreamed about for some twenty years. It appeared from time to time in my mind, but only as a romantic idea.

Finally, one day I decided that I would do it. I could not spend any more time of my life without even trying. I had let the years fly. No one has their life assured and postponing it more was practically burying it.

So, I went from a wish to a decision. Then I began to share that dream, to discuss it with my family and other people. And so, in December of 2015, I shared with my friend Enrique my transatlantic longing. My words resonated with him, because he also wanted to do it. Perhaps without being aware of it, we turned that very conversation into a goal. We established that we would sail to America before the end of the following year, in November of 2016.

If I had not decided to turn that dream into a decision and from there into a goal, maybe it would still be only imagination. However, here I am, a year after having fulfilled that dream, achieving another one: this book that you now have in your hands.

With your dreams the same thing will happen, if you make the decision to go after them and apply the points that I have suggested. I know that you are not alone in the journey you want to make.

As in my case, there are people who also want to live what you imagine. Maybe right now you can think of someone, but even if you have no idea who might be interested, it doesn't matter. The important thing is that you make the decision and start talking about your dreams.

Then, turn your dreams into goals and take your first steps. You will be surprised to start discovering that there are others with a sailor's spirit who want to embark on projects like yours. When you convert your dream into a goal, you start by writing it down and begin sharing it with others, because you know and believe that you will do it. People with the same ideals will listen to you and begin to form a team that will make up your crew of sailors.

The young sailor who was part of our troop followed the advice we gave him for the dizziness and, thanks to that, the next day his situation improved. The color returned to his face, his stomach began to calm down and his thoughts stopped playing with the idea of giving up. When the nausea disappeared, he rejoined the daily tasks, lived with us and had the experience with his five senses intact.

In the evening, we had spaghetti a la marinara with parmesan cheese and salad. For dessert we ate ice cream, which some of us had with a hot coffee and others with an aromatic tea.

Later, from the deck, we observed on the mast a hawk that was solemn and regal, illuminated by the light of the moon.

THE MAJESTY OF CREATION

3rd Nautical Day 11.12.2016

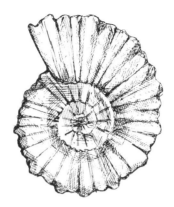

We continue sailing 220ºS toward the islands of Cape Verde to look for the trade winds[5]. The only way to cross the Atlantic with the power of air is to take advantage of the vigor of this transparent current that starts in southern Africa, climbs toward Europe and glides over the Atlantic toward the west in the direction of America.

Some people assume that spending so many days in the middle of the ocean is boring, that seeing only water and the blue of space is the daily repetition of the same video, but it's not like that. Every morning is different. The sky changes its staging all the time, at the whim of the clouds. Occasionally, you observe gigantic and fluffy cumulus

---

5   The trade winds are a current of air that blows from subtropical areas of high pressure (southwestern Africa) to the equatorial regions of low pressure, toward the west, that is, toward America.

clouds; other times, you look at the light and aerodynamic trail of cirrus like wakes of a multitude of airplanes. In addition, the color of the sunrises and especially of the sunsets, gave us unimaginably spectacular shows—a view impossible to match with brushstrokes in the hands of artists, or digital images from the best programs that a computer can offer.

I often got up early to have the joy of observing the sunrise and how its rays colored with warm tones each of the clouds that floated in the morning sky. Feeling that current dashing into your face while you make out a multicolored horizon that, little by little, is displacing the darkness until it becomes fullness of light, is an incomparable gift. What price can you put on breathing the beginning of the day with a cup of coffee in hand, the sea breeze and a sky that transforms at will?

The sunsets, which I personally like more than those beautiful sunrises, emerged glorious. Each evening was an impressive light show, which recreated lights and tonalities only seen by the eyes of a sailor. Mixtures of pink, violet, red and other shades of wonderful intensity. They are moments that elevate your soul and make you see how small we are and how grand creation is. And when you think that this beauty ends with the entrance of the night, a myriad of stars that dress the sky await you.

On the sea, the night shows you the unique communication of the planet. Before the flashing message of the celestial bodies, the waters of the ocean respond with phosphorescent flashes of marine plankton. An incredibly brilliant combination illuminates the surface of the sea in shadows with its phosphorescent points. There is a silent and visual chat between space and the waters. It is as if the stars were blinking toward the sea, and this were returning the wink with a green and glowing signal. *My eyes witnessed an encounter of luminous language between the vaulted ceiling of the sky and the basement of the sea.*

Given this, it is impossible not to size up the immensity of the universe and the perfection of the planet. To perceive how everything works with an exact and interlaced order. From the cells of our organism, to the orbit of the earth and the planets around the sun. The entire universe coordinated in perfection. Observing these immense celestial bodies, which from below resemble tiny fireflies, show the wonderful work of creation.

Living those moments allows you to understand that we are a pinch of sand on the earth. Nevertheless, despite being aware of how small we are, you understand that you are there, that you are part of the spectacle, not just a spectator, who, when crossing the ocean or the mainland, are part of this wonder called life. There in the sea, in the middle of nowhere, or maybe, in the middle of everything, I understood that the monotony is not in our circumstances, nor in the events we face, but in oneself, within us, in our mind.

When we lose the ability to feel wonder, and take for granted the greeting of friends and colleagues, or despise the "good morning" of our wife, the conversation with our children, and we stop savoring every food we taste, then we live a routine. That's when every day is identical. The reason for the boredom is that we have lost the capacity for observation and the virtue of gratitude for the small everyday details.

If we focus on looking carefully at what surrounds us, we will always find beauty. Invariably, we will discover that there are beautiful situations and moments at all times and regardless of where we are. Life is not monotonous, but we can become monotonous. This is another of the lessons that the sea gave me.

The greatness of the human being

We human beings are part of the miracle of creation. You and I are an integral part of this universal mechanism. Unfortunately, many of us have forgotten that we are a perfect design. And I do not say this only with regard to the wonder of the functioning of our body, I mean everything that had to coincide so that we would be born. We are not the work of chance. We were created with a purpose and for a reason. Maybe you haven't thought about it before; but for you to have life and be who you are, it was necessary for millions of combinations and special circumstances to happen. Let's reflect on this.

At birth, each is the latest model of several generations. In addition to being unique and unequaled, we are the fruit of an unrepeatable combination. In order for us to be born, our parents had to meet, that is, to get together in the same place at a certain time. If one of them had not attended the party where they met, for example, we would not have been born. In addition, it was necessary for them to come to an agreement and have an intimate encounter. If that moment had not occurred or had been postponed, the union between the sperm and the ovum from which we emerged would have been different and the result would not have been us. Added to this, for us to exist it was necessary that the paternal and maternal grandparents had their own meeting and that our parents were born from there.

The probabilities for this to happen as it happened are endless, because remember that the chain of marital unions continues back eight generations of great-grandparents and so on. Doing a little math and if we follow the family tree for hundreds or thousands of years, literally millions of people and circumstances were required to have coincided in a moment in time and space for us to be born. A single variation in this chain of encounters and you and I would not be here.

There is something more to add to this complex network. For our conception, the sperm that formed us was required to beat between one and two hundred million competitors that sought to fertilize the same egg. We are the consequence of the strongest and fastest of our father's gametes at that time. Do you realize that you are unique, unrepeatable and part of a perfect design? Do you understand that it would be impossible to program a system that controlled all the combinations that were needed for you to be born? This tells us that you are an extraordinary being, that is, out of the ordinary, uncommon. It is impossible for there to be someone like you.

It is impossible for me to think that someone born of such an extraordinary combination was born without a purpose. Just as each star has its place in space, so you have yours on the earth. You are here to achieve goals, to contribute, to give your light to others and with it, to fulfill a plan that began thousands of years ago.

Did you know that the plankton, those aquatic organisms that I saw at night showing their brightness in the waters, are microscopic organisms? Each of them is imperceptible to the naked eye, an apparent insignificance of the planet, but by joining others like themselves, they perform wonderful functions, from allowing other living beings, such as whales, to feed, to delighting sailors with their spectacular brilliance. That's how we people are. Before the majesty of the universe, we are like a leaf of a tree that falls in the immensity of the forest; nevertheless, **we have a task to accomplish, a mission to live and goals to achieve.** Nothing in this world is insignificant; everything has a reason for being. **There is a reason why you are here.** What you need to do is discover it, and this starts by recognizing that you are special.

Many of us grew up under circumstances that made us believe that we are not worth anything, but we are not a mistake, we are part of this wonderful world that gives us the opportunity to shine. Write your list of personal qualities and keep them in mind. I'm serious. Take a pen and write down your virtues. Consider any of the qualities that you identify in yourself or that others have mentioned to you that you possess, including those that you have not believed to be true.

Develop your talents in freedom

I know that for some it is difficult to believe that they are valuable. I understood it better during the months I lived in Japan. There I had the fortune to learn about the wise and profound culture of that country. On one occasion, Asami Sam, one of my Japanese colleagues, invited me to dinner at his house. There he had several small trees in small pots. On some occasion, I had seen them in Spain, but at that time they were not as popular as they are now. So, because of curiosity, I asked what species they were and what those dwarf trees were called. He replied that they were known as "bonsai" and that they were not a different species, and neither were they dwarfs. They are trees that grow from an ordinary seed. Their size is due to a process applied to them during the beginning of their growth. Part of this work is to prune their roots and branches, to surround and cover the root with a metal mesh and to place the plant in a small pot. That is where its name comes from, since bonsai means potted tree.

This is what happens to many people, unfortunately. We are all born from a seed with the potential to be leafy oaks; however, in our beginnings we received information that prunes our roots. We hear that we must settle for our circumstances; that it was our lot to live like this; that we will study to be employees of others; that we will never succeed or even that we are useless, lazy and stupid.

Like "bonsais" our branches are pruned and our dreams are encased in pots from which we think we will never leave. We even come to believe that we were created to be in those vessels and bury our longings next to our roots that have been cut. We become "bonsai people", potted men and women.

Maybe we received a limiting education, we grew up in a family with scarcities or we had really adverse circumstances. All of this set limits in our mind and we adjusted to the size of the limiting expectations of that moment. But there is a great advantage that we as people have: We are not trees, we have the ability to change. We cannot change the past, but we can transform our present and with it the future. *You can recover and exploit the seed you were born with. That potential remains in you.* It is a matter of releasing the moorings that have kept you on the shore, with the desire to sail on the high seas, or living inside a small vessel.

Everything starts by recognizing that you are not a dwarf tree—it was just your lot to be in a small pot—but now you can get out of it. You can break the metal mesh around your thoughts and recover your true nature. You have the power to stop being an ornamental plant and to leave for the forest or, as we sailors say, to row out to sea.

I am a faithful believer that the human being has no limits when he gets passionate about an idea, when he recognizes that he is a unique being and with a seed of greatness. Do you think it was your lot to grow in a pot? Do you think you have more potential than what you are using? Are you willing to let your roots and branches grow? Are you convinced that you have a seed of freedom, a seed of a sailor?

I invite you to make a list of the qualities you have. Write down each characteristic that distinguishes you, be it the talents you were born with or the skills or virtues you have acquired. Look back and identify everything you have learned despite the limitations you had during your childhood and youth. Do you see it? There is the potential, the capacity to train you. You have branches and roots that are anxious to develop.

In addition to the characteristics you have written down, ask people who know you to share what they see in you. You can consult family, friends and co-workers. Do not be afraid to do it. It is important to give ourselves the value we have, because he who values something, cares for and appreciates it more. Remember, you are not a coincidence; you are special, and you have a purpose.

THE MALAISE

4th Nautical Day 11.13.2016

As of today, we have sailed 460 nautical miles. The sea continues the same as yesterday. We have changed the course from 230° to 270° to find better winds. This day started very well. The sky appeared friendly, totally light blue with light clouds scattered here and there. The pleasant temperature, around twenty-four degrees centigrade. At night, the thermometer did not fall below eighteen degrees.

To celebrate this good start of the day, we had boiled potatoes with green beans and grilled chicken breasts. The crown of the beginning of the day was that, thanks to technology, I telephoned Pilar, my wife. After exchanging greetings, news and mutually informing each other that both of us and the rest of the family were doing well, I told her some of the stories I already had from the trip and we had a good time despite the distance. It is not easy to be away from the family for a long time, but each situation has a price to pay.

What restrains our desires?

That is reality. Embarking on a project or setting out to achieve our dreams has a price to pay. The price of an endeavor begins to be paid even before starting it. It gives the impression that life is infatuated with stopping us; as if circumstances suddenly worsened to prevent us from taking the first steps toward our desired destination. This has happened to me not a few times. It is as if there were a law of life that tried to discourage us when we made the decision to sail, to launch out into an important project. *All it takes is for us to start dreaming, and others, circumstances or even ourselves, build impediments.* There are many examples and I am sure you have experienced several of them.

As soon as we set out to save, unexpected expenses arise. If we are ready to start an outdoor exercise routine, the sky closes in and the rain appears. Maybe you have tried to start a business and the people close to you tell you that it is a bad idea, that you will not succeed. Dreams not only detonate our enthusiasm, they also awaken waves that can frighten us. Nevertheless, we must remember that it is just that, *the challenges,* which *indicate to us that we are on the right path.* If there were no challenges to face, then what would be the value of the goals? That is why, not everyone revives their navigator's heart, for fear of facing the adversities or the tides that you discover and learn to navigate when you are out on the high seas.

The days before our departure, I experienced a challenge that was about to lead me to give up the voyage. Our departure date was set for Wednesday, November 9. The members of the team had agreed to meet at the Port of Las Palmas one day before to coordinate the final details. The previous Sunday, being at home with almost everything ready to leave, I began to feel in bad health. My stomach ached, I lost my appetite and suffered constant nausea. The pain spread to other parts of my body. The malaise was such that that night I was forced to go to the emergency department of a hospital.

The doctor didn't find any physiological cause for the discomforts. He prescribed some pills for stomach ailments and sent me back home. My expectation was that, with the taking of the medicines and a good rest, I would wake up well. The next day the situation remained the same. My body didn't respond favorably. The lack of appetite, nausea and pain remained out of reach. The next day I had to fly from Madrid to the island to leave, and my body was screaming at me not to do it. I thought maybe that day I would find myself getting better. Pilar showed her concern when she saw me in those conditions, even though I minimized the malaise in front of her.

On Tuesday morning, I woke up with the same symptoms. I pretended to feel good so as not to worry my wife and took the flight. That night, in a nice restaurant, we the crew got together. In addition to having our last dinner on terra firma, we reviewed our tasks, the responsibilities of each person and several points of the crossing. My appetite was still absent, and the malaise did not subside.

At the end of the gathering, I approached the friend with whom I had planned the trip from the beginning and told him how I felt. I informed him that if I woke up the same, I would not sail with them. Despite the disappointment, he understood my situation and tried to reassure me by saying that what I decided was fine.

I went to bed, hoping to wake up in better health, but it wasn't like that. It was time to make the decision. *My common sense and good judgment told me that, in my fragile state of health, it was not prudent to go to sea for more than twenty days, far from the mainland.* What if I worsened? What if it was a major health problem that was just emerging? Would I be a burden for the rest of the crew? Would we have to interrupt the trip or call for help? What would happen to my family? However, on the other hand, my sailing spirit was fighting a battle with my common sense. *Are you going to miss this adventure? Will you have another chance in life to carry it out? Do you have an illness or is it fear that afflicts you?*

Now I understand what was happening in that defining moment. Fear was taking over my body and, subconsciously, my mind. This is what happens when we risk the safety of our comfort zone. The fear of risks, of breaking the routine, of leaving the shore, shows up. Our dreams are dreams because they break the limits of everyday life, they go beyond the borders under which we have lived. Taking the step out of there, produces fear.

We are educated to move within certain rules, just like tennis players do. The court is the territory within which players must keep the ball in order to win. If they get out of there, they lose the game.

In life, we grow up under an education that establishes lines within which we must perform. Going outside those limits means failure, although in fact, *it is outside the game field where the most valuable and transcendent desires that we have are found.*

This is why dreams start as a fantasy. They are something that we think of and that we believe would be good to do at some point, but since they are outside the common territory, we postpone them. Without realizing it, we don't allow ourselves to take the ball beyond the court.

This is how my desire to make the crossing of the Atlantic on a sailboat began. Since a long time before, I had dreamed of making this trip, maybe more than twenty years; but in reality, it was just that, a figment of the imagination; an idea that I intended to make happen "at some point."

When we reason like this, what we have is just a fantasy. We imagine and idealize something without really setting out to do it. Fantasies can last for years in our minds without ever materializing, because they are just that, chimeras, simple imagination. They are romantic and idealistic ideas with which we have not committed ourselves. Wishful thinking. It is like a seed that we have in our barn, but that we have not sown. Of course, it starts with them, without seed there can be nothing, but if we water them with fear, instead of blossoming, they will never germinate; and if fear leads us to not even attempt to put them in the dirt, we will continue to live in the inconsequential comfort zone.

I took the next step in December 2015. That's when that idea that I had harbored so long would become reality. I turned my fantasy into a decision. The difference is that deciding contains fuel, gives you energy, leads you to take actions. It is the equivalent of taking the seed out of the barn, sowing it and starting to water it. Now that yearning is no longer stored in our mind, but begins to grow, to have a life of its own. It is there when we share it with others, we talk about it, we look for opportunities; we think about it more regularly and it stops being an occasional thought to become something important, a priority. In the period of the decision, we still do not know how we will do things, but we are certain that we will find a way to achieve it.

Interestingly, a few months after my resolution, I found a good friend, another sailor, who told me that he had acquired a thirty-nine-foot Lagoon catamaran. That same day, we determined that in November we would make the crossing across the Atlantic. The seed had germinated, and its small stem began to show small leaves of life. When we make the decision to undertake what we purpose to do, circumstances and people begin to appear that help you get closer to your dream. I do not think this is magic or something mystical. I believe that this power arises because our level of commitment increases and now we are more attentive; we look for and perceive everything that is related to the project and, therefore, it is appearing. In making the decision, we know that God will provide what is required, since we have put forth a higher level of responsibility and commitment on our part.

From that day and for the next six months, my friend and I had many conversations. We inquired about how to make the trip; we consulted other sailors; we shared it with friends; we researched on the Internet and opened the invitation to other sailors to increase the crew. We had expanded the size of the tennis court and now we were playing under new rules. However, moving to the next level meant not only rallying on a larger court, it required us to leave the stadium.

The answer lies in the determination

And now, here I was, mere hours before sailing, feeling badly and doubting if I would get on the boat. The fantasy had become a decision, but now one more step was lacking, **determination.**

This is the great difference between yearning for something and realizing it. It is what makes fear stop being a brake despite feeling it. You can revoke, adjust, change or postpone a decision; but with a determination there is no going back, come what may. With determination, we do everything to make the plant grow and bear fruit, we will not let it die. To determine is to take on the total conviction of and commitment to what we have decided.

I cannot find a better example to define determination than that of another sailor, Hernán Cortés.

This Spanish adventurer and conqueror transcended circumstances due to his resolution. The history books mention him as a key piece of the Spanish extension in America. During those turbulent times, Spain established colonies in the Caribbean, Central America and what is now Mexico. Cortés rebelled against the Spanish governor located in Cuba, given his refusal to let him go and conquer the Aztec territory. When, in rebellion, he arrived in Mexican lands, he "burned" the boats to prevent his crew from changing their minds and renouncing his undertaking. The message was clear: ***"When you determine to do something, there is no turning back."***

I understood that I would not live my adventure while it was a fantasy or just a decision. To live it, I needed to have a fierce determination. I had to face that fear. It was then that I decided there would be no going back. A sailor does not have a rearview mirror; everything is forward, no matter what happens. I would make the crossing. ***The malaise of my body would not become my brake; I would burn the ships. My friends would not leave without me.*** In the same way, entrepreneurs must have determination. Daring to start a business or any company implies firmness and courage. Before this, the most we can hope for is a decision. It's when we make up our minds, when we do not consider the option of stopping, or returning. That's when things are done, when adversities are faced, and the gears of action begin to work.

The big day arrived, and my body woke up as sick as the night before. I showered, got dressed, had a coffee and toast with jam and went to the port. As I approached the ship and saw its name *El Impulso* written on the side, I understood that I had made the right decision. In my physics class, I had learned that impulse is the force that moves a body to go forward or backward. With respect to my person and my determination, everything would be forward.

A couple of days after I set sail, my body worked perfectly. I understood that fear had made me its prey. A fear manifested through physical discomfort. Yes, fear, even when we think we don't feel it, works in us to stop us. Getting out of our comfort zone causes us anguish.

The same thing happens with each new endeavor that we start. Whether it's a job change, giving the engagement ring, quitting our job to start our business, having a child or moving from town, what we're doing is getting out to sea. And delving into unpredictable waters produces doubts; but in spite of that, we have to uphold our decision and navigate toward our destiny.

Your life cannot be stopped by that feeling of uncertainty that a change generates. Remember that, ***if we continue doing the same thing, we will continue living the same way.*** Advances and improvements occur when we modify what we do and how we live. We can identify these signs in our minds and even in our bodies, which warn us that we are taking steps toward the unknown, or at least, toward a place where we could have little or no mastery.

Despite being a sailor with many years of experience,

during the days before starting the crossing of the Atlantic, my body refused to board the ship. The same can happen to you at the mere thought of making an important decision. Do you want to leave the firm ground of your current job? Are you tired of the poor results you have in your business? Do you want to move to the next level in your love relationship? Do you want to fill your life with new experiences and emotions to give it more meaning? Then do not obey fear. **Get out of your comfort zone, climb aboard your *El Impulso* and sail out to sea.**

I invite you to make a list of the things that instill fear in the face of the idea of embarking on the journey to pursue your dreams. To make it easier, answer the following questions:

1. What do you think can be lost if you launch yourself out to your sea?

2. What are the chances of what you fear really happening?

3. Is there anything you can do to reduce the size of the risk?

4. What is bigger, your dream or those risks?

CHANGING COURSE,
NOT DESTINATION

5th Nautical Day 11.14.2016

Course 223°. Winds of ten to fifteen knots and speed of five knots. The sky appeared with clouds and clearings. The ambient temperature was 24°C. Our position at noon was latitude 22° 23′ N; longitude 25° 02′ W. During the night, the wind and speed dropped to two knots.

At 8:30 a.m., we decided to change course and let out the asymmetric spinnaker. We oriented it with a 270° course, with which we increased the speed to five knots. We removed the Genoa and lowered the mainsail.

When the winds are very calm, the above maneuver is the alternative in order to increase speed. Of course, to achieve this, you have to make a change in the course, so as not to deviate from the objective and then modify the course again.

Although it is known that the shortest distance between two points is a straight line, applying this rule on the sea is not always so advisable, because you have to rely on the force of the wind, and that is where you play with the combination of the sails and the course. The same thing happened on the third nautical day in which, having left Gran Canaria, we descended toward Cape Verde to take advantage of the trade winds. Whoever sees what we were doing on a map would think that we were heading in the wrong direction, because this African island country is located south of the Canary Islands, our starting point.

The apparent detour was part of our navigation plan. It was essential to travel in that direction to take the impulse that the strong trade winds would give to the sails of our boat and thus, move toward our destination. We knew that, even if we lowered a little, the wind that we would find there would drive us with more vigor toward the Caribbean. This movement on our route shows me a similarity with life.

There are no shortcuts to success

Throughout my professional experience, I learned that the shortest route is not always the best way to approach the goal. *Often, you need to take unwanted, but necessary, roads.* Sometimes you have to skirt near the coasts to avoid turbulence, and resist the temptation to sail in a straight line, thinking that it is the shortest way forward. In fact, *if you want the force of the wind to direct you, you need to change the direction of the sails and your route regularly.* Although in distance the route is longer, it will not be in time and mainly, in protection. But the time comes when you need to get away from the shore. You cannot stay there. To have security forever is stagnation, it is to stop growing; breathing to survive instead of inhaling gigantic puffs of pure air in the middle of the ocean. The daring actions and risks are what allow us to learn, those that add centimeters to our height and expand the heart. By witnessing new horizons, the mind opens, and with it, growth takes place.

Somehow, ever since my childhood, God deposited in my inner being that longing to leave the port and embark on a journey to know the world. Getting away from the mainland, that is, from the comfort and the known, was a growing desire in my inner being ever since I was a child.

Every summer, at the end of the school year, my parents would take me to a village in the Sierra de Ávila. Coming from the capital, the life of the countryside was different to me. In that place, the work revolved around agriculture, so I learned about natural processes.

They harvested the wheat by hand, forming circular heaps of more than ten meters in diameter, with the ears extending outward. For threshing, threshing boards pulled by mules or horses were used. Many times, I had to thresh mounted on one of these animals and go around and around until the goal was achieved.

Later, with the grains released, everything was shoveled upwards so that the wind separated them from the straw.

With my eyes wide open, I observed how most of what was obtained from planting was unusable for human consumption. Lots of chaff and little grain. The entire job lasted for days. If we add to this the amount of time from the sowing of the seed until the day we collect the ears, we are talking about months. An impatient person was not suitable for this job.

Like the process to obtain the grain of wheat, in life **only those who dare to enter processes where comfort and indifference are threshed out, will achieve success.** To succeed in our ventures we need, on the one hand, to get away from the port and, on the other, to take action, exercise our patience and, often, be brave. I have seen it throughout my decades of life. For example, of the nearly eight hundred students who started the course in nautical sciences, only eighty of us finished it. Some chose to be grain, others stayed glued to the head or even, the wind took them like straw.

Another similar situation is that in the almost thirty years that I have been a professional in my network marketing company, I have seen that it is a handful of people who, willing to go through the process demanded by any company, stick to the phases that allow them to prosper. Many start this type of business. Some of them leave, others remain and keep surviving, doing a little here and a little there, working well for a while and then forgetting to do it, and only a few dare to undergo the whole process. The air arrives and the grain is still stuck to the ear and the opportunity to have clean grain for the flour is lost, or at least, postponed.

This great alternative of distribution in network marketing demands that you prepare yourself, that you read, that you learn to be an entrepreneur. It also asks you to develop others, to train people, to be a leader. And it is there where a certain number of people choose not to go through the natural process of growth that is required to be a good leader. Many expect to earn millions in four or five months. They want to have fruits without even having worked the crop enough. They want flour, but they are not willing to work the necessary process to have it. But we will reflect in detail on leadership later on. For now, I want to make clear that, to reach our goals, we must strive. Sometimes, change the route, but not the destination. We need to work, be patient and stay on course.

All of the above shows us that success requires that a price be paid. But this cost becomes insignificant when the size of the dream we pursue is much larger. Turning wheat grains into delicious pieces of bread is more valuable than the hard work involved in reaching it. When you have in your mind where you want to go and really want to be there, the route changes do not defeat you. They may discourage you a little, but when you remember your goal, good energy envelops you.

It makes me laugh to go to a supermarket and see the great variety of breads there are. We go through the bakery and take it for granted that, as always, there will be enough loaves on the shelves. We forget that behind each piece, there is a long path of actions, people, animals, machinery and technology that have had to stick to what nature dictates so that bakers or industrial flour producers produce that food. *There is no fruit without previous sowing and effort; there is no success with shortcuts.* Life is governed by natural phases. Although the method I encountered in the Sierra de Ávila was native, it worked, and taught me that if we want something we must do what must be done, even if it takes time and energy.

Sometimes, we forget that people are part of nature. The current life, with its great technological advances, makes it easier for us to eliminate from our minds that we come from dust and we go to dust. We are subject to natural laws and *we need to go through processes that separate our grain from the chaff.* And although life itself is sometimes responsible for introducing us to situations that thresh our character, we must act and take action to strengthen and develop ourselves. Remember that, just as the boats have to adjust their route according to the wind conditions, we need to modify the plans and the way of doing things from time to time to reach our destination. We change the route, not the destination.

Starting new challenges requires leaving the shore, learning from others and understanding that there are processes to follow in everything. The experiences that I lived outside my daily environment broadened my perspectives on work, hard labor and the satisfaction of results. When I began my university studies in Santander and Bilbao to obtain a degree, my horizon was broadened. There my adventurous spirit was reflected in several activities that I carried out.

I remember that my father was surprised when I told him I wanted to study nautical engineering and that the only option was to move to Santander, about four hundred kilometers from home. His immediate response was to question why study a profession of the sea if I had never lived on the coast. I guess he was unaware of the great impact on my life of that trip he took me on when I was five years old. Since then, the sea had remained in my mind and heart.

Despite his surprise, my father supported my desire to study that profession. So, I moved to Santander. To cover my expenses, I worked in the afternoons in a government office and in the evenings—in the company of Dan, my Dutch friend—we sang popular songs in the nightclubs. This second task, of course, was more rewarding than the first and made us popular among the young women; a non-monetary benefit that we also considered part of the pay.

Studying and working at the same time is a little complicated; but when we have a passion, nothing stops us. I had treasured that desire for the sea for many years and true desires, sooner or later, find an outlet to become reality. Going to the Nautical School was the first step to remove the lid of my dreams and walk toward them. I know that, like me, you have important yearnings. Perhaps you have hidden them with the day to day, responsibilities, habit or comfort. However, I'm sure they continue within you; they rest calm; but all it takes is to blow on them a little so that they light again the burning coal of what they have always been. The energy that these desires give you will not explode until you stop skirting the coast of tranquility and settling for the ordinary. *If you want to grow, it is essential to expand your horizon.* Sometimes, this will involve changing jobs, starting your own business, leaving home or even leaving your homeland. People do not develop while remaining the same. A simple way to force ourselves to go further is by leaving that comfort zone. Stretching generates pain, produces uncertainty, but detonates our capacity. That is the way of entrepreneurship.

Leave the coast to discover new oceans

Being entrepreneurs means leaving the shore and going out into the ocean. This is what happens when we give up being employees and start our own projects. I know because for many years I was a salaried employee. I admit that I was happy, because I worked with Spanish and international companies, I sailed the seas and went to many countries. I earned enough money, I enjoyed working at my leisure and I did it, for a while, at sea. But one day, after twenty-seven years of working for others, I grew tired of not enjoying the freedom to be my own boss. It was true that the income was good, the positions important and the companies in which I worked, prestigious. Despite this, the time came when I felt like I was inside a beautiful cage, in which I received good food and shelter; nevertheless, I could not go beyond those silver bars. Do not get misled. I am grateful to each and every one of the bosses who gave me the opportunity to collaborate with them, and put their trust in me. I enjoyed the work. But there comes a time when you recognize that the good is not the excellent and that the favorable does not necessarily satisfy your dreams. We reach the limit when we are overtaken by the need to go further, to enjoy freedom, to live in fullness.

If you have a sailor's heart, maybe these words are shaking your inner self. Maybe you are going through a moment of mental fatigue like the one I had. You want to start your own project; to have more control of your time, your life and your money. You want to spend more time with your family and live the day based on your priorities, not those of others. If this is your case, then you have a call to leave the coast; to separate your grains from the head and start your voyage. Surely, thinking about it produces mixed feelings; on the one hand, the idea excites you, but on the other, you are afraid of making a mistake and failing. But I ask you: Which defeat is greater, that of trying and not reaching the goal, or not even trying?

The educational system and the family tradition in which many grew up slows down the sailor spirit. We learn from childhood that success is studying to get a good job, earning as much as possible, ascending to prestigious positions and retiring at sixty-five. I grew up with that in my mind. As a child, I thought that the best thing for me was to become a great executive. And at twenty, I was already one of them. At that age, I headed a team of twenty-five engineers in a textile industry project in Japan. In the eyes of everyone, including my own, my life was a professional success. After that, my career continued to rise. Actually, I consider myself a privileged man in terms of my experiences and work achievements. However, the spirit of a sailor turned out to be bigger than the economic benefits, the positions and the recognitions. At forty-five and against all the logic of what I learned about professional success, I burned my ships and started a project that was going to give me freedom. I have been in it since then, and through it I have crossed more seas and enjoyed what I longed for: controlling my time, my life and my money, spending more hours with my family and living each day with my priorities, not with those of others.

Being independent and undertaking a personal network marketing project was a radical change in my professional life. In the eyes of many colleagues, friends and family, it was crazy and even a mistake. They had not understood that I was not changing my goal by an inch. On the contrary, I was aligning my sails with the flow of the wind. I had modified the route, but not the destination. In light of this, dear navigator, arises one of the most relevant questions that a human being should ask him or herself: **Where do I want to go? Where am I directing my boat?** In short, are you clear about your destination? If so, congratulations. I suggest you write it down. Do not leave it in your mind, start to take it out, to share it. If you still don't know where you're going, it's time to define it or at least start doing it. Return to the list of dreams you made at the beginning of this book.

Review them and define which one of them or perhaps, which ones are the most important; those that you cannot fail to achieve. Surely, there you will find the course that defines your destiny.

PERIOD OF CALM

7th Nautical Day 11.16.2016

Our location is latitude 22° 09′ north and longitude 27° 02′ west. We have been three days with calm seas and very gentle winds; on occasion, we could even say there is no wind at all. At 12:00, a little wind came in. We are traveling in a southwesterly direction 240°. At 13:00, the wind died down and the sea remained in the doldrums[6]. The previous days, the wind was scarce and therefore, the distance traveled was not what we wanted. We continued in the right direction, but at a very low speed.

This happens in the sea and especially when you sail with sails, because you depend on the will of Aeolus. If this god of Greek mythology decides not to blow, the

---

6   The doldrums is stillness of the wind in the sea. Tomas de Berlanga discovered this archipelago by chance, when en route to Peru in 1535; the doldrums paralyzed his ship.

best antidote is patience and a good attitude in the face of the circumstances. That's what we did during the calm period. We took advantage of the stillness of nature to fish, swim in the middle of the ocean, sunbathe, read the books we had, spend time together, have socializing times, play dice poker and do some minor repairs on the boat.

On the sixth nautical day, with the ship stopped in the middle of the Atlantic, we bathed in the ocean. Swimming there is a special experience, because you know it's impossible to hit bottom. We were three thousand meters from any support and wrapped in the most immense crystalline sheet you can imagine. However, you cannot believe that you are in the middle of the ocean, because it behaves like a pool. Even the temperature of the water was wonderful, approximately twenty-four degrees centigrade. We were in the most gigantic pool in the world just for us, shared with thousands of marine species that swam invisibly below and around us.

Learning and applying is the key to success

In the performance of a job, and especially if you are an entrepreneur, *it is necessary to have moments of calm to strengthen the relationships of the members of the team* and invest in ourselves, in our growth. This is one of the points that many professionals forget, and therefore tend not to stay up-to-date and thus, they lose good results. A group of collaborators requires moments of relaxation together. Of course, these periods are brief, but they allow the relations to be strengthened.

One of the many things I learned during my stay in Japan is the importance of playing together. The inhabitants of the place arrived before the clock-in time to exercise and recreate in the sports facilities of the company. Within days of seeing how the Japanese colleagues behaved, I motivated our team to do the same. This helped us to favor our bodies, start the day with more energy and mainly, to spend time together outside professional responsibilities. The fact that we played tennis, racquetball or just spent time together in the gymnasium, allowed conversations to take place that usually did not occur during work hours. Also, at work there should be times of calm that should be taken advantage of.

A sailor requires this type of activity to relax, share and unify the crew. The voyage is not only to reach the goal, but to enjoy the journey and live together. Interpersonal relationships are a fundamental part of life. As I mentioned, in addition to the gatherings, we also took advantage of quiet times for reading and maintenance tasks and repairs.

Reading good books is one of the keys to stay up-to-date in the world of work and expand our way of thinking. In business and personal growth, making room to update ourselves in our field is essential. In fact, in the network marketing industry, **one of the keys to developing leadership and growth in the business is to keep reading.** Those who do not, simply delay or even stop the expansion of their business. But this is not exclusive to this world. It is also applicable to traditional jobs and companies.

I developed an anxiety about studying as a child. At school, I strived to be among the students with high grades. My grandmother was my motivator in those years. When I returned from school I lived with her, since she lived in our house. Occasionally, there were no great conversations, but she was there. In the afternoons, I sat at the night table[7] to do my homework while she prayed the rosary. My feet played with the tablecloth that hung to the floor. When I felt cold, I lifted it a little to feel on my legs the heat radiating from the brazier placed under the table.

My grandmother would give me a snack of a couple of pieces of bread with oil and sugar. But her greatest influence on me was to make me believe in myself and in my potential. On a regular basis, she encouraged me to continue striving at school. She said that my greatest strength was my willpower, my tenacity for trying hard in studying, for doing more than others. Her words are still fresh: "Son, do not worry about the time you spend learning; that is going to put you in one of the first places."

Now I see the importance and the encouragement that her words gave me. She believed in me and she made me do it too. My desire to learn has not yet disappeared and since I was a kid I liked to share what I was learning. I took every opportunity I had to learn. When I was ten years old, the washing machine that we had at home broke down. Since money was not something we had to

---

7 A round table with a platform where a brazier can be placed; it is usually covered with a long tablecloth that reaches to the floor.

spare, I knew it would take a while to pay a technician to fix it. Thinking that if I took the machine apart and put it back together again, I would not damage it more than it already was, I dared to try to repair it and I did it. For me, doing it not only involved helping my parents, it was also a good opportunity to learn. The summers I spent in the Sierra de Ávila I took time to teach mathematics, Latin and French to other local children. I continued to dedicate myself with seriousness to studying, which served me not only to finish the course with good grades, I could also do my professional internships with CAMPSA, the first Spanish company in the oil industry, which allowed me to graduate as a nautical engineer.

As I was always attracted by engineering, I studied, read and practiced it to continue learning; however, my interest in education was broadened thanks to an invitation from my wife. Just as I had a preference for science, she had a preference for literature and human development. On one occasion, when I was working for a multinational petrochemical engineering company, Pilar asked me to accompany her to a conference on the topics that interested her. I attended. The speaker turned out to be Eduardo Criado, an excellent advertising agent, playwright and speaker. His talk, promoting Dale Carnegie's tools of human relationships, impacted my life greatly and made me value, for the first time, the importance of personal relationships. After the exposition, Pilar and I enrolled in what would be my first course in the world of human development.

For six months, every Monday for four hours, we delighted

in learning from the speaker how to get along with people, how to get their attention, avoid and resolve conflicts and other relevant aspects of dealing with people. I started to apply the concepts I learned in my work. The results were very good. In fact, among the two hundred engineers who worked together in the engineering company, it was me who got two promotions that year. I am convinced that, in addition to my technical knowledge, my new leadership ability made the difference. To my hunger to learn technical matters, I added the desire to know more about the world of personal development and leadership.

Since then, I have not stopped attending courses and workshops, listening to lectures and reading. I have invested time and money in it, and with greater intensity since I started our business. I am convinced that this preparation and our commitment to work have been the main causes of our company's success. In fact, the whole team has the instruction to read a good book every month. In addition, we listen to conferences and organize and attend training events several times a year.

Find your mentor

Another alternative to maintain growth is to have mentors. From my perspective, it is the fastest and most effective way to learn, because you do it by watching and listening to those who already know. In fact, this is how we learn when we are babies. With our eyes wide open, we observe what our parents, aunts and uncles, grandparents or our older siblings are doing and talking about. In childhood, we learn very fast because we don't question our mentors. We do what they tell us without hesitation. When we enter school, we hear more voices, and in adolescence, we question what we have learned, and we allow ourselves to be influenced by new mentors that appear; whether from the sphere of our friends, opinion leaders in the media or a teacher.

Later, in our professional life we also learn thanks to people who guide us. Of course, this requires an essential element called humility and taking an attitude of apprentices, not know-it-alls. Remember that ripe fruits rot. When we think that there is nothing left for us to learn, we are in a process of putrefaction. Having mentors is an act of wisdom that will take us faster to the top. It is the student who chooses the teacher, not the other way around. That is why it is important to know how to choose one well.

Some ideas to consider in choosing your mentor may be their knowledge and experience in the area we want to learn; the confidence that he or she transmits to us; that they are a person who inspires us, thanks to their integrity, transparency and consistency. That is, what they say and what they do are the same and they are a person with high and clear ethical values.

A good mentor does not impose his opinion, but teaches and makes the student discover for himself the answer he is looking for. *In a healthy relationship of educator and apprentice, there is harmony and generosity.* Some alleged mentors or rather, manipulators disguised as them, exercise intolerance, envy, arrogance or abuse over their students. This type of people you have to flee from, because in reality what they seek is not to share what they know, but to satisfy their own ambition and achieve their own objectives, belittling others.

It's amazing how all ideas flow freely when you have moments of calm such as those offered by the sea these days. During the time of reading, play and recreation, I have remembered the great mentors that I have had throughout my life. Experienced engineers who didn't hesitate to share with me their knowledge about the sea and the great machines of the ships. In the business, I have received great teachings from many valuable men and women, dedicated, generous, talented, professional, creative, dreamers, with clear mission and vision and sure of their destiny.

Sunning on the deck, I reflected on these people who have sown their time and wisdom in me. I'm grateful to them for having done it. I invite you to make a list of the people that are valuable to you, who have been your mentors and, if possible, contact them to thank them for what they deposited in you. On the other hand, *if we are still alive, we need someone else to teach us.* I suggest you make a list of the areas in which you want to improve. Maybe it's your health, finances, the practice of a sport, your role as father and husband, a job, your spiritual life or in your professional role. Next to each growth area, write down the name of at least one person who can become your mentor. Remember to consider the characteristics that a mentor must have and that I mentioned earlier. Finally, ask those people to let you learn from them. I can assure you that, if they fulfill the qualities of the mentor, they will be happy to do so.

In addition to this, do not forget to attend courses and trainings, to listen to lectures and to read. ***The one who prepares, prospers.*** Life is a cycle and to date, I have been able to mentor many sailors, including my own children. Nevertheless, we must have the wisdom and humility to know when they, our mentees, require and choose other mentors. Instead of lamenting and letting our ego betray us, we should be grateful for the opportunity we had to be part of their formation and successes.

TURBULENCE AND SETBACKS

10th Nautical Day 11.19.2016

We began the day with wind and calm waters. After what happened the previous days, having a calm time again is appreciated. We took the time to make some repairs to the equipment. We improved the state of the windmill that produces electricity. The problem was that it didn't generate as much energy as we wanted. Ingenuity emerged, and we strengthened the vanes with the rigid covers of my notebook, covering them with plastic to protect them from humidity. We also repaired some breaks that the asymmetric spinnaker[8] had, as it had been damaged a couple of days ago when it became entangled in the Genoa[9]. So we went to work on these tasks and improved the conditions of various tools,

---

8   The asymmetric spinnaker is a type of nautical sail of triangular form with the sides of different length.
9   This is the name given to the largest and most important of the triangular sails of a ship, located in the prow.

since on the eighth nautical day we had an incident that warned us to check every point and tool of the boat.

That day, our position at 10:00 was latitude 22° 14' north and longitude 27° 52' west. At 13:00, wind began to come in from the stern in favor of our 270° course. We got to a speed of between 4 and 5 knots, with the sea slightly agitated, but with its gentle consent to sail. We ate boiled rice with fresh tuna and an abundant salad of lettuce and tomato. Everything looked excellent, although we wanted more wind to reach our destination on time.

There are moments of our existence that flow like the days of calm on the high seas. Everything seems to be in order, our income stable and the situation with the family also. The winds blow in our favor and if things continue this way, everything indicates that we will sail without setbacks. The sun shines and the clouds do not foretell storms. Under these circumstances, it would seem that we live a beautiful story with a happy development and ending; a fairy tale where witches and sorceresses do not participate.

But nothing in life remains the same, everything changes, situations are modified, the sun is hidden, and the colors of the horizon are no longer seen. Too sweet to stay the same forever.

Life gives us tests

At about 19:31, one of the crew members informed us of

an emergency. Water was pouring into the bilge[10] of the starboard body of the catamaran. If we did not resolve the leak immediately, the consequences would be catastrophic. The water was entering and adding more weight to that side of the now fragile vessel. We had to resolve the situation in a few minutes. All the members of the crew went into action and coordinated our actions to avoid the worst.

Immediately, two people got the manual pump to take out the water; three teammates formed a chain to remove as much of the water as they could with buckets and two other crew members threw themselves into stopping more from coming in. They closed the bottom faucets. For a couple of seconds, we thought that the situation was resolved, but it was not; ocean water continued to leak in.

In my mind, and I think in everyone else's mind, there was no alternative but to resolve the situation. Our arms moved resembling the choreography of a Broadway musical, only that we were not in a theater, but in the middle of the Atlantic.

Time passed and we could not find a way to beat the pace of the water's entrance. It was gaining on us. My companions increased the speed at which they passed the buckets full of water; we pumped as much as we could. We didn't stop even for a second to take a breath

---

10 Lower cavity of the ship in which the different waters that enter the ship meet through pipes and then are ejected to the sea by means of pumps.

or relax our muscles; there was no time. We became pumping machines.

Suddenly, we heard the shout of a companion cheering us: "Let's go! Keep going!" Suddenly and without thinking, I heard myself calling out more encouraging words: "Come on, we can do it! Don't give up!"

Minutes later, which seemed like a couple of hours of anguish, the crew assigned to find the cause of the flood, found it. The hose from the water pump intake for the sewage treatment had come loose from the clamps that held it. They closed the intake and the liquid stopped coming in, so they proceeded to fix the fasteners.

With happiness greater than our fatigue, we continued to remove the water using the manual pump, another electric pump and the buckets, until we completely dried the bilge. When we were done, and due to the discipline of recording the important activities in the logbook, I looked at the clock. It was 19:58. Only 27 minutes had passed!

Having the situation under control, we realized how exhausted we were. The adrenaline began to disappear little by little and for a few seconds we exchanged glances in silence, communicating the satisfaction of having worked as a team and saving our lives.

Suddenly, laughter emerged and the jubilation continued until several minutes later. We went above deck and the sky delighted us with the wonderful spectacle of the stars on a moonless night. We had just resolved a situation of such gravity that we felt as if we had reached a great goal. Teamwork paid off. God supported our effort and now He was congratulating us with the deep blue vault, saturated with tiny sparkling points.

They say that after the storm comes the calm, and that night we all experienced it. However, in our case the pleasure would not last for long. The water leakage challenge was resolved, and we were able to rest both emotionally and physically, but that peace lasted only a couple of days.

Today at 22:00 hours a downpour arrived that was becoming rough weather. The rain began to fall with force on the boat and the sea was getting rough. What had been a quiet pool a few days before turned into a saltwater blender. **The waves grew to a height of more than six meters and the wind blew at seventy kilometers per hour.** Every sea wave that rushed toward us looked like a building that would fall on us.

It is just in these moments when experience becomes a wonderful counselor. Four of us had a lot of it for all the years of sailing. We knew that you do not fight the sea, but that you respect it and allow it to show its power. We only had to do what the navigation manuals indicate for these circumstances, not to lose calm and endure the storm. Due to the high wind speed we proceeded to curl[11] the mainsail to withstand the bad weather. Thus, with the

---

11 This maneuver consists of reducing the volume of the sail, sticking it more to the mast to reduce the impact of the wind against it, and thus improving the stability of the boat.

sail minimized and taking turns on watch, we endured the storm.

The similarity with life is evident. ***Although we have periods of stability, they will not last forever,*** and especially when you dare to leave the port and venture into the undertaking of new projects, into going after your dreams, the storms appear.

Dear sailor, do not expect only times of calm seas. Remember that adversities are part of the growth process. The one who dares to break their comfort zone has two things guaranteed: The first is that they will have new experiences and the second is that they will face adversity. The positive side of both is that they help us learn and grow. In addition, even if we decide not to go out to sea, we face challenges. We can continue in our comfort zone and suddenly we receive a negative medical diagnosis, we lose our job, or we lose a loved one. This is life. If in any case we will have challenges, I prefer to wrestle with those generated by pursuing our dreams.

The importance of the team

Keeping calm and relying on your team is the key to dealing with the storms. That's what we did in the face of the inundation and during every storm and tempest we went through. In the face of adversity, we didn't lose our calm, but we delegated the responsibilities. Everyone focused on what was up to them and we all collaborated. Without this level of respect and participation it is not possible to undertake a project successfully.

In the crossing through the high seas, teamwork is not only required for emergencies, but also on a day-to-day basis. For each day, we all had a responsibility to attend to. On several occasions each of us had to wash the dishes, prepare the food, take night watches, clean clothes, clean the boat and even restrict the use of water during our personal hygiene.

Without the constant cooperation of each crew member, the trip becomes a nightmare and possibly a failure. The same happens in our professional and family enterprises. When we all collaborate, we join efforts and allow each person to use their talents, *and when working as a team, we increase the chances of success.*

Remembering my childhood, I can say that the first time I experienced effective teamwork was with my friends from the neighborhood where I grew up. When I was little, we moved to a community that was created for government employees, since my father worked for them. It was a place of lower middle class, but nice and where I got a good group of friends. One situation we experienced was that, to go to school, we needed to cross through an area of less fortunate people. The kids there did not view us favorably. Each time we passed through their territories, the risk of being persecuted and even attacked was imminent. Those of my neighborhood nicknamed them, "the neighborhood of the rogues." When I was on my way to school, I was running through those streets.

On one occasion, I suffered the consequences of going alone, because they overtook me and gave me a good beating. Of course, I was not the only one who had this problem. The other children in the area also suffered from it.

One day, tired of the situation, my older brother and a friend of his age decided to create a gang to defend us. They thought that joining together and forming a front was the alternative in order for them to stop bothering us. So they took on the task of integrating several boys into their clan. I would not stay out for any reason, so I joined the group. The team was forming and growing. We even created our membership cards for the gang. Besides being a fraternity to counteract the enemy, we had fun together. We played soccer and we slipped in without a ticket to the stadiums of Real and Atlético.

Regarding the dangerous neighbors, on several occasions we had warrior encounters with them. We decided that we would not allow them to continue bothering and intimidating us. They had to see that we knew how to respond and that we were willing to fight. The strategy worked. After a while of facing them, they stopped bothering us. Unity made strength. From that moment on, I understood the importance of partnerships and team-building. **What I could not achieve alone, I achieved jointly in collaboration with other people.** Of course, on that occasion, the objective was to protect me from the abuse of the children of the other neighborhood, but I had understood the value of association.

When I started my professional life, I was clear that promoting unity with my colleagues and collaborators would lead us to obtain the results that the company required. A lone sailor will not have the extent, nor the magnitude of the achievements that he obtains when joining other adventurers like himself. In all my professional jobs, I always pursued teamwork.

In our company, collaboration between partners is essential. Without it, you do not get anywhere; however, if you know how to cooperate, negotiate, make agreements and allow others to have benefits like you, then we all prosper. I have experienced it for a long time. It is a technique or process that does not fail.

Working like this has allowed us to have businesses in many countries, to my good fortune and that of my family. How could we do that without the participation of other people? How big would our company be if we had not developed others and trusted their abilities and talents? Would we have the capacity, energy and time to serve entrepreneurs in so many nations? Of course not. Only if you have a system that promotes working like this, can you grow at these magnitudes and even more.

I mention the importance of the system because in traditional companies, you can focus on working as a team, but your collaborators may not. The results don't happen and they receive their salary anyway. But when the business model and, therefore, the results of each associate, depend on collective work, on exercising a service leadership, then things progress, as has happened in our activity.

If you are willing to pursue your dreams, it will be important that you choose whom you will associate with and establish a work process that relies on collaboration. Of course, I do not necessarily mean a legal partnership, although it could be that way in some cases. I'm saying that you need to be part of a team that protects you, encourages you and helps you get further than where you can go alone. That is why there are unions, chambers and institutions of doctors, lawyers, businessmen, merchants and artists. Teamwork is what makes network marketing businesses work so successfully.

Something practical that you can do right now is to write down who the members of your team are. Next to the name of each of them, write their qualities and areas of expertise. Having this will give you a clearer perspective of how your team is formed and how to distribute tasks and responsibilities. It will also allow you to know how to divide the work in the most effective way in times of turbulence. If you still do not have this team, then make a list of the people you want to invite to form it to promote each other.

For all the above reasons, for me teamwork is one of the central rules of life, because it helps you protect yourself and have professional achievements. In addition, when you are in the middle of the ocean and water leaks into your boat, it allows your friends and you, in collaboration, to come out ahead of the inundation.

Nature rewarded our patience, dedication and teamwork by removing the storm and offering a starry sky and a water cradle full of luminous beings who, once again, chatted with the stars. In addition, God gave us a pat on the back, by giving us the sight of a few shooting stars.

THE BEST CREW

12th Nautical Day 11.21.2016

L ocation at 11:12 hours: latitude 24° 51' north, longitude 36° 01' west. We advanced all night to the west at 270°. We sailed with the main and the genoa in donkey ears[12] with stern winds. At 9:15, we changed direction to 290° to catch more winds from the starboard quarter. The sky was cloudy and we expected some showers. Before the rain came, we launched four lines of fishing rods. At around 13:00, several fish had already been caught. The best we got was a striped tuna weighing about ten kilograms. We put it in the fridge because we had already planned oven-roasted dolphinfish for the meal, accompanied by potatoes with vegetables and to start with, a gazpacho.

---

12 Navigation technique with stern wind (from the rear of the boat), with the Genoa oriented toward a band and the mainsail to the opposite side. This navigation gives an open and light course.

We did not fish for sport, but to feed ourselves. Although we carried provisions, it is not advisable to feed only on them, because, as you don't know the behavior of the wind, the route may take more days than expected and you may be left without food.

Business financial intelligence:

As entrepreneurs, we must do the same with our company. It is not wise to take our company's resources to "eat" daily. It is essential to have provisions stored in the pantry. In our culture, many start a business and want to immediately have the income generated, and what happens is that they eat up the seeds of the first fruits. They do not reinvest in the business.

In the economic area, two factors are very important: One is to *invest* in your company so that it continues to grow and generate wealth, and the second is to *save* to have good reserves for times of need. Saving is a virtue of few people, but salvation in critical moments for those few who practice it, applying financial intelligence.

We Latinos, in general terms, lack this virtue and, for this reason, we suffer the consequences. One invests in a business, especially at the beginning, and we should not believe that as soon as we start it, we can withdraw money for our daily expenses. To do so is to slow down its growth and, as a consequence, to postpone or, failing that, to eliminate its future.

In my case, I started saving capital since I was young.

The first of my married years was a period in which I also did it. After getting married, we enjoyed a wonderful honeymoon, as it lasted three months. When you work in shipping companies, you spend a lot of time at sea, therefore, your rest periods are long.

At the end of the romantic holiday period, I joined my professional life outside of Spain almost a consecutive year. During that period, our marriage relationship became an epistolary relationship. We wrote love letters constantly. It was the alternative we had to communicate. It was not easy, but all that time it allowed me to save a significant part of my income. One of the advantages of being at sea is that there you do not have options to spend your money; although people are creative to produce ways to squander. Certain crewmen gambled their income in games of cards, bets and all kinds of games. When we arrived at a port, I watched as some comrades spent their salary without care. My purpose was to save. It is a practice that I have maintained throughout my life. I find it very advisable to do so, because that money becomes an important support for difficult times or when opportunities arise.

I suggest you do the same. I have never met anyone who has regretted doing it. I know that many times our income is low compared to the expenses we have; nevertheless, even in those moments it is possible to save, even a little. Saving is more a habit than an economic possibility. **Do not underestimate what you can save for the future, even if they are small amounts**; I assure you that with time you will be surprised at what you have accumulated. Also, in times of need it will be a balm that softens the hardness of those days, or when the opportunity of an investment comes, you will have the resources to do it.

I was writing about our fishing and from there I went on to comment on savings. This distraction, after all, led me to touch on a relevant topic; because savings really are. In married life, it goes without saying, money is a weighty matter. I don't mean to say that only prosperous couples can have a good marriage. We all know people who have a lot of money and who are not happy, or have even divorced and sometimes are on very bad terms. Nevertheless, the management of finances is one of the most important components in life as a couple.

The family: value and foundation

When thinking about the relationship of a couple, I remembered how important Pilar has been in my life. We have been married more than fifty years. I have lived more years with her than with her absence. All the adventures, undertakings and professional changes would not have been possible without her great support. A few days ago, I was able to communicate with her; it was her birthday. In addition to congratulating her and wishing her the best, I shared with her about our progress. They were very pleasant minutes. She also told me about some of her activities, how well our business progresses and informed me that the whole family was in good condition. It was the best way to start the day.

We have lived through all kinds of situations together.

We have overcome challenges. We enjoyed good events and fun times and we have faced strong adversities. Our sea has sometimes surprised us with strong turbulence, but we have stayed together, trusting each other, supporting each other in difficult decisions. We continue on board and with a wonderful family crew.

I'm sure that making a team with your family, but especially with your partner, is the most rewarding thing you can do. ***There is no better team of collaborators for the journey of life than your own family.*** On the days of the inundation and the storm, I reflected on the importance of working as a team; but there is no association more important than the one we make with our partner.

I met Pilar when I lived as a student in Santander. She lived in a nearby town. One of the summers, instead of returning home to Madrid, I stayed at the residence of a friend of my father where they were hosting people. It was a really nice palace. The guests were working people who for some reason did work for a season there. I took care of some administrative activities and in return I had a place to stay. It was a pleasure to be in that place, not only because of the palace facilities, but because I enjoyed it very much; it was a place where it was easy to have fun. I lived with other young people, we went to the beach, there were happy holidays. I had a great time. That summer I met Pilar, but I saw very little of her, because she went to spend the holiday period with family in France. Although she caught my attention, we didn't have the time to spend with each other.

The following summer, I asked my father to let me stay again in the same place. On this occasion, Pilar did not go on vacation to another place and we spent more time with each other. We had fun around the town, on the beach, at meetings and started a friendship. After the holidays, I stayed in Santander, but as an irony of life, she moved to study law in Madrid. So I was in her homeland and she in mine.

We maintained our relationship through letters and eventually we got together. Now that I remember our life, I see that the postal service played an important role in our communication. I regret to a certain extent that the new generations, like my grandchildren, for example, do not experience the special feeling of receiving a letter. Although unquestionably, sending an email, a text or *WhatsApp* message is something wonderful, incredible and immediate; that emotion that we experienced when receiving a missive, was something very special. We should, from time to time, send a letter by mail to our loved ones and especially to the youngest, to give them the opportunity to feel what we got to experience.

Anyway, I remembered that Pilar had moved to Madrid to study and I had stayed in Santander studying nautical engineering. At the end of my course, I left for almost a year to do my internship. Again, our relationship was maintained through ink and paper. Upon my return, at twenty-two years of age and the degree completed, we got married. Since then, we have worked together, with wonderful moments and great challenges, but always together. ***Our partner is the main association and the***

best teammate that a person can have. Your partner is the most important of all the people with whom you will navigate through life. I, without the participation, initiative and support of Pilar, would not have had the achievements that I have achieved, both in the personal and family areas, and professionally. Simply put, it would have been impossible.

It is clear to me that many people are not choosing their partner well, or maybe they are not clear that this partnership requires a lot of teamwork. I know it is not easy to share a life or your projects with the wrong person. Hence the importance of making this choice well; but we also have to realize that in all group work we must each contribute a high degree of respect, tolerance, yielding and completing the tasks that belong to us; just as we did on *El Impulso* on the voyage.

One issue that seems to me important to consider in order to strengthen and extend the bonds of the couple, is the difference between love, falling in love and physical attraction. No couple's relationship will last long sustained only on the fleeting sentimental and even fantasy desire of falling in love. Neither will the effusiveness and beauty of the bodies sustain a marital society for a long time. Bodies deteriorate, emotions change, adversities appear.

Falling in love is the period in which, more than seeing the reality of the other and our relationship, we let ourselves be guided by the enthusiasm of being together; by physical attraction; by the sensations that we experience and that lead us to think about the other almost all the time. It's something pleasant and even fun, but extremely fragile, as fleeting as physical beauty or the spectacular sunrise on the ocean that vanishes in a few minutes. Couples who want to sustain their lives on either of those two factors, live at risk of breakup, or at least very high frustration.

Given this, *it is the commitment of love and mutual respect that makes this team remain united.* Respecting the other implies letting them be who they have wanted to be, instead of trying to make them become the person we want them to be. When we understand that true love is one that goes beyond our emotions, that it involves the will and the reason to respect our partner, to continue giving them the place they deserve despite time, physical changes, adversities and even the eventual diminishing of the emotions; it is love that sustains a couple's relationship through time. That love is even what helps us make decisions that prevent emotions from disappearing or cause them to flourish again.

I always knew that the most important thing in my life was my family. I set out to give primacy to my wife and children and to maintain my goals. I love my tribe madly. It is what makes me feel alive and inspires me to keep going no matter what, being an example and empowering them to also achieve their own dreams. When you team up with your wife and family, the bonds are strengthened.

When my children flew from the nest, they spread their wings with great force. Not only did they leave home and Madrid, but they moved, each of them, out of Spain; even beyond Europe; they left for another continent. One went to live in the United States of America, another in Chile and one more in Mexico. Despite this, the unity did not break apart.

A great help has been the fact that our business allows us to travel, without problems, constantly. So, when they were on the other side of the ocean, Pilar and I frequently boarded a plane to visit them. Maybe you think it's the economic capacity that maintained the relationship, but it's not like that. A family can be close, even live together and not have unity and mutual support. The force of the habit of team building since they were small has turned out that now, grown up and with the happiness of having given us grandchildren, they live in Spain again, near us. They joined our company and have been very successful.

Turning your partner and your children into a real team implies love, but also work and having clear priorities. Whoever does not put their family first, is very likely to end up losing it. The one who places their personal interests above those of the rest of the team, will end up losing the group and with it, also many of their goals; because, as I mentioned before, **we cannot achieve great goals if we do not have the mutual support of one another.**

Selfishness is an annihilator of teams. Do you remember, dear sailor, that I shared with you about the gang that we formed in the neighborhood? We succeeded as a group to confront our enemies and to have fun; however, when the founders and leaders, my brother and one of his friends, began to fight for their own interests, for trying to do only their will; for wanting to be the only leader; the egos collided. The gang dissolved.

In the family, in our company and in any team, it is essential to put aside our selfishness. If we believe that we alone are right; if we constantly strive to do only what is our suggestion and ignore others and try to deny them their rights to participate, to give their opinion, to have the same opportunities as the rest, we will be digging the grave of the team. On *El Impulso,* the crew members knew that we should have a cooperative attitude. You cannot cross the ocean with a group of divided people. In the sea of our lives it does not work either.

Today we turned back the clock an hour to adjust it to the time zone that we are in. With this, we are three hours behind Spain. After the meal, we received an unexpected gift. This gift became the happiest note of the day. We received the visit of a young and nice whale who was playing with us. It came to the surface by the bow and then by the stern. It swam happily around the boat. It really had fun with us; it seemed to be reveling in our "oh", "yes" and other expressions of enjoyment and surprise. It crossed below the ship and emerged from the other side. It spun around, showed us its white belly and then opened its impressive mouth in front of us. It was wonderful to watch the giant mammal have fun with us. It delighted us with its clowning around for about two hours, enlivening our sailing and leaving us with a strong spirit. It said goodbye, opening its mouth like a smile and with a flutter of its tail like "See you soon."

MID-VOYAGE

14th Nautical Day 11.23.2016

Our location at 11:12 is latitude 24° 47′ north and longitude 41° 03′ west. We continue heading 280° northwest. The winds are of medium intensity, 25 knots. The speed of the catamaran is between 4.5 to 7 knots. The sky is full of clouds.

Throughout our voyage, we had very few sightings of other boats, but today we saw two. At 8:30, we saw a sailboat with a 230° course cruising at great speed, advancing with an engine. At 15:00 hours, we spotted a five-masted cruise ship that was heading to Saint John, in the Caribbean.

Each ship contains many stories. If they also saw us, in a small sailboat, in the middle of the Atlantic, they could have imagined what we are on—an adventure, a voyage of pleasure, risk and human challenges, or maybe we went unnoticed. Such is life. We each have our situations, achievements and challenges. We navigate through life without realizing that the person next to us has just lost a loved one; the driver of the car next to ours is getting married tomorrow; the girl who is running through the park will have a little brother and the slender executive at the next table is processing her divorce. In the ocean of life, we cross paths with other sailors, each with their history, with their planned route, or simply floating in the middle of the sea. Some starting their journey and others are about to reach their destination, even if they had not planned one.

That reminds me that yesterday we covered half of our trip and with the distance traveled; we have a little less than 1,350 miles. We reached the point of no return on the thirteenth day of the voyage and our plan is to cover it in twenty days. The windless times delayed us; nevertheless, we expect better winds that will allow us to move faster.

Goals

Reaching the halfway point is like reaching a first goal. Of course, at sea, the middle of the voyage does not allow you to stop, because you continue on the ocean. Nevertheless, knowing that you reached the midpoint gives you a sense of accomplishment, of knowing that you are approaching your destination. For that reason, during dinner yesterday we toasted and celebrated. We had a small party that strengthened our enthusiasm to get to Martinique. This partial achievement gave us a second wind for the rest of the route.

There are moments when I am on watch, especially during the beginning or end of the day, when I reflect with great astonishment on what I am living. For years, I longed for this trip. For a long time, it was just an idea, a "maybe"; but now I experience it, I am living it. I find myself as the protagonist of a dream come true. I perceive myself in the middle of the Atlantic, receiving the wet breeze drops that come from the water cut that our boat opens. There is nothing above me, only sky. The silence is interrupted from time to time by the cawing of a bird. It is incredible to have one more purpose that I have fulfilled in my life.

I review my existence and I realize that I am and am not privileged. On the one hand, I see that I have had wonderful experiences, a family and a wife that have given me many happy moments. Nevertheless, as a counterpart, I also understand that I have achieved what I have and have experienced what I have also because of the decisions I have made and the actions that I have carried out. *It is impossible to achieve goals without willpower.* Now I see that my grandmother's belief that I am a headstrong person has helped me a lot along the way. Both in my jobs, as in my personal life, as in my business, it is what has allowed me to succeed. I don't believe that luck is what defines people's lives, but rather the measures that we take and what we commit ourselves to.

I compare the fruits of willpower with an example I read in a book by Michael Gerber, *The E-Myth*[13], which I call

---

13 Gerber, Michael E. *The E-myth: why most businesses don't work and what to do about it.* New York: HarperCollins, 2012.

"the fat guy and the skinny guy." Imagine a person sitting comfortably in an armchair in front of the television. It's Saturday afternoon. On the screen there is an athletic competition. This man is impressed by the vital strength and skill of the athletes. In the meantime, he's eating a sandwich, the second one since he sat down to watch the game. He is absorbed in what happens in the contest, when suddenly his friend appears, dressed in sports clothes, and invites him to exercise. "Come on, come with me, it will do you good! In addition, you really need to move your body, you are overweight, you should exercise, at least do it for your health."

The man, still sprawled out on the sofa, responds that on another occasion he will. However, in his mind he revives the desire to do so. Inside, he projects a thinner image of himself, with more muscles, healthy and active. The big question is whether he will. Acting on it or not will make all the difference. So, in the face of any kind of challenge, we have those two options, which I call: "the fat guy" and "the skinny guy".

The skinny person is the one who uses and lives with words like "discipline", "exercise", "organization". He doesn't tolerate or allow concessions in the face of what damages his goals. He is a lover of details, a type of tyrant with himself. He cannot be still; he needs to be in constant motion. He lives for action. When the skinny man enters the scene, we must be alert, things will start to move, circumstances will change. If it's about food, he starts eliminating the food that hurts him; he removes foods high in fat and sugar from the pantry and refrigerator.

He leaves home to buy a new pair of sneakers, shorts and a sweatshirt. Things are going to change, he's going to improve. He has just taken on a new commitment with himself.

The skinny man plans a new regime of life: getting up at five in the morning, running regardless of the weather to reach five kilometers; taking a cold shower at six; having breakfast with toasted whole wheat bread, a coffee without sugar and half a grapefruit. Going to work on a bicycle; going back home at seven in the afternoon and running three more kilometers. Going to bed at ten o'clock at night. The world starts to be a different place!

The skinny man keeps practicing his new routine. In a short time, he has lost a kilogram and goes to bed dreaming of winning the Boston Marathon. Why not? The way things are going, it's a matter of time, of keeping on doing the same things.

A few days later, his weight decreases by another half kilo. He is becoming a weight-loss machine. He continues with his routine and decides that it is time to go the extra mile: an extra half hour of effort in the morning and a little more in the evening. He can no longer wait to get on the scale. Eagerly he goes to the bathroom. Full of expectations about the diagnosis of the device, he looks at the scale. Nothing! He has not lost an extra kilo. His weight is the same. Discouragement begins to appear. The few grams that now appear are of resentment. "It cannot be; nothing, after so much effort, sweat and sacrifice? It's not fair!"

But he doesn't think about giving up, even though he now feels something different, he does not know what it is, but he perceives something in his being that does not please him.

The next morning, he wakes up at the same time thinking about continuing to work hard. It's raining outside and it's a bit cold. Inside, he still experiences that strange sensation he experienced the night before. What is it? There is someone else in his body and his mind, it is the fat guy! He has come back and doesn't want to run! What's more, he doesn't even want to get out of bed. Run? In this cold? The fat man doesn't want anything to do with all this.

Minutes later, the fat guy is in front of the fridge looking for something to eat. After so much effort he deserves a prize, an exception. The marathon no longer occupies his thoughts, the slimming machine has vanished, the sweatshirt, the shorts and the sneakers are no longer used. The fat guy is back and has put his mechanisms into action.

This tends to happen to all of us. It can be with losing weight, improving family relationships, studying, saving or the dedication we put into our work or into our company. I have seen and lived it in my own activity. When someone starts it, they start like the skinny guy, are passionate, dedicate time, invest energy and even money. But the fat guy peeks out when some obstacles begin to appear: you place an order and the products do not arrive on time; some people you invite reject you or even your relatives tell you not to waste your time, that you will never prosper. Other fat people infect you with their closeness, their words of discouragement, their despair. Their pessimism, disguised as reality, strengthens the fat guy.

Part of the problem is that we do not realize that both exist in our person; it is our struggle between the conscious and the subconscious or our dualistic mind that often conditions us to make excuses and to lose opportunities. We tend to believe that when the skinny guy is in control, it is us. In the times in which we advance, we discipline ourselves and do the right thing, we are convinced that it is the "I" that is making the decisions. But when the fat guy awakens and we return to the previous lifestyle, we also believe that it is the "me" that is acting, but it is not so. It is not the "I", it is the "we".

The skinny guy and the fat guy of this metaphor are two totally different ways of thinking and acting. They have opposite needs, interests and lifestyles. They do not like each other, one cannot be in the presence of the other. In other words, when we let our skinny guy take control, we are pushing the fat guy away and vice versa. Anyone who has experienced this internal conflict can recognize what I mean. We cannot be both at the same time. One of them must win and in doing so, the other will be defeated. They both know and are aware of it.

Reaching goals is impossible for the fat spirit. Its nature drives us toward comfort, toward the easy, toward the known. It invites us to join with others like us, without hope, without plans, with lives stuck to the shore or confined to the port. It is the attitude of the skinny guy that will take us to a new destination. It is that spirit that allows us to gather the strength to break the routine and initiate a different way of life.

Living our adventure on the ocean could only be done thanks to that skinny guy of the crew. The sailors cannot afford to have the fat guy come back. He continues to exist within us, but we keep him away. When he appears, it is time to ignore him, to jump into action, not to think. Do not let your fat guy talk to you, and when he does, do not listen to him! The worst thing we can do is get into a conversation with the fat guy. There is no negotiating with him; he is simply to be rejected. None of his offers is advisable; he will never lead you out to sea, or to the ocean full of endless possibilities. Every day of our journey, we have responsibilities. If we did not meet them, it would be difficult to reach the destination; and even if we did, it would be an unbearable journey full of complaints, indifference, disputes and unhappiness.

Who are you obeying now? I suggest that as soon as you identify that the fat guy is approaching, avoid him. Do not let adverse circumstances place the fat guy in the lead. On the contrary, it's precisely when there are challenges that we need to act like the skinny guy. It is that part of us that helps us to get ahead, to prosper, to keep us on the boat, despite the storm, and gives us the character even to face down a mutiny.

Identify in what areas or moments of your life the fat guy

usually appears. Be clear about it so that when those moments come, you will take opposite actions. For example, when you notice the fat guy approaching, call a skinny friend; go out to do a productive activity; get away from the temptations of the fat guy.

As for the rest of our day at sea, today we ate stew of cooked vegetables and the delicious tuna that we caught the previous day. At 16:00, we spotted two whales. It was a real delight to observe them amongst five-meter-high waves. The day passed without great news, except for the detail of the whales and the increase in wind speed to 28 knots. This allowed us to have an average speed of 6.3 knots and move faster toward our goal, toward our destination.

The Importance or Magic of the Number Three

17th Nautical Day 11.26.2016

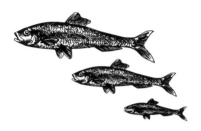

Today I started my watch at 00:00 hours. The sea was calm, and the wind was slack. The speed of the boat was four to five knots. We sailed with the mainsail and the genoa, centering the wind by the starboard quarter and heading toward our course of 256°. At 12:00 hours, the ship's location was latitude 23° 55' north and longitude 45° 21' west.

At 14:00 hours, we spotted a boat on the starboard quarter about four miles away. It was a Spanish sailboat named *Airatea* that was sailing to the island of Antigua. Until this time, the wind was still light, but began to rise reaching twenty knots. The sea remained calm. This combination increased the speed of *El Impulso* and our hope.

At nine we had breakfast. The day was wonderful, and the sun shone with all its brightness. Our view stretched for miles and the temperature was perfect. The catamaran's advance continued to be positive. At 8:00 am, we furled the genoa and took out the code zero sail. By staying that way throughout the nautical day, we traveled one hundred and forty nautical miles. A good progress for the day. During the day, we fished a good catch. Actually, this success was due to the use of probabilities in our favor. What we did was put four rods in the stern.

The greater the number of actions, the greater the possibilities for results

We applied a principle that, as such, works in different aspects of our life. The more actions we take, **and the greater the number of our activities and alternatives, the more likely we are to succeed.** On several occasions, we had put out only one or two rods, and the catch had been little or none. However, every time we set up four fishing rods, we got some fish. The lesson is simple; nevertheless, I am surprised that many people go through life without taking it into account. I will offer a couple of examples in this regard.

The first example is one I have experienced and applied in our company. In it, through contacting people, we create networks of consumption and distribution of products. The bigger your organization is and the more active your members remain, the greater your income. However, as often happens in any enterprise, over time, a percentage of the people who are associated decrease their level of commitment and ability to work, and others even stop marketing, consuming or serving their own community.

There will always be someone who listens more to their fat personality than to their skinny side.

In any business—and this is no exception—we have the certainty that there will be a turnover of people. Therefore, the more associates you have in the organization, the more likely it is that the number of those who remain will be greater. *If you have the foresight and the discipline to set up more rods, you will catch more fish.*

My experience in the network marketing project has taught me—and it is what I teach my partners—that for companies to be productive and profitable, they have to strike a balance between the amount of turnover of stock and the composition and number of network members. I present the example of the femur bone and the muscle. The bone would be the turnover of an organization, but a bone that is not protected by good muscle—which would be the network of people—will always be very fragile and exposed to any breakage; that is, be subject to loss of turnover. In summary, balance your company.

If you devote all your effort to a small number of distributors, or as we say in the jargon of network marketing, only one or two lines of distribution, your business will be fragile. Therefore, to be successful in this type of company—and I dare say in any other—it is fundamental to offer the opportunity and the products to as many people as possible.

Those who get good results in sales don't do so because all of the proposals they make to potential customers are accepted; of course not. They are successful because they are the ones who contact the most prospects. They set up as many rods as possible; they understand that by doing so, they increase their chances of obtaining fruits.

The second example I want to share has to do with the money we earn. The most common way a person brings capital into their home is through employment. If we do not take into consideration the law of probabilities, what we do is ensure that one hundred percent of our income depends on a single source: our work. If we are responsible for financially supporting the family and all the money we receive comes only from there, the risk of reducing the income to zero is very high. Any day, our boss can come up to us and say goodbye. At that moment, our only water tap is closed. If we only set up one fishing rod and the line breaks, we run out of fish. And if we add to that the lack of savings, we will be in serious, very serious, problems.

This is why being entrepreneurs is so important, especially in this era where technology is replacing the workforce at an alarming rate. Starting a business of our own that allows us to generate another income in addition to our employment, is to throw another hook into the sea.

Of course, I recommend doing network marketing as a business, because I know it is a wonderful alternative. Both my family and I have enjoyed its benefits for many years, and we also have economic security for our future. Any opportunity to generate legal income is one alternative; but the selling of products with our distribution system is an even more excellent one. This type of entrepreneurship is like casting a group of fishing lines at the same time, or rather, like casting a whole network of them.

In our current century, there is a current or fever that encourages us to be enterprising, especially toward young people. I love the idea. It is what is required in our nations, to increase the number of people with entrepreneurial vision. Unfortunately, **ninety-six percent of those who start a business project fail less than ten years after starting it**. As if this wasn't enough, some of them can only sustain their company for a very short time. If we're going to open a business and we don't want to be part of that statistic, we have to think and act like three different people and have three points of support. The fact that the number three is a constant in several fields is very interesting.

The three mentalities of the entrepreneur

Throughout my life, I have learned that this number has a special, almost magical, function, especially with regard to balance. For example, for a round table to be firm, it requires at least three equidistant legs, with an angle of one hundred and twenty degrees. The way astronomical navigation works to know the location of a ship at sea is by taking three stars or planets as reference. Within the fundamental commandments of sailing is the fact that you must not set sail without having three important elements: drinking water, food and fuel. In addition, you know that you will be subjected to frequent sudden movements, heeling and swaying, and to cope with them, you require three points of support: both feet with legs wide open, and an arm to lean on some part of the boat. If you don't do it like this, you will trip, fall and even feel dizzy. All of this can result in accidents of major consequence.

In companies, the number three is likewise very important. Remember *that there is turbulence in business and if you do not have support points, you will lose your balance.* The types of business shocks are: 1) changes in the market and customers; 2) changes in technology and increase in strength and 3) level of competition, to name a few.

If we want to undertake something, the first thing we should know is the following: Who am I? What are my talents? What experience do I have in the professional field? Then comes the question: In what area of entrepreneurship would I like to develop? Or how could my current situation change with respect to the future? But we must be aware that in the business world, and above all, in small businesses, which are the most abundant, 96% of those that start fail before 10 years. This means that only 4% stay afloat. The important thing is to understand why this happens.

Experience has taught me that in the world of entrepreneurship, there are three points of support to avoid these pitfalls, and that there are three fundamental roles that must be played. The key factors are: the mind, the heart and education. And the three personalities or mentalities to be executed are: **the entrepreneur, the manager and the technician**. In the book, *The E-Myth*, by Michael E. Gerber, I found clear concepts that coincide with this perspective. Adding my experience as an entrepreneur to that book, I will begin by explaining the three different fundamental activities for those who wish to succeed in their project.

Let's look at the **entrepreneur** first. Having such an attitude is what turns any situation, however trivial it may seem, into an exceptional opportunity. The entrepreneur is the visionary within us, the dreamer. It is that part of us that allows us to see beyond the ordinary. When we are in this mode, we have enough energy to act, take action and motivate others to do the same. It is the flame that ignites the fire, the catalyst for change. An enterprising person lives in the future, is innovative by nature, creates new methods to enter markets and seeks to be on the same level as the world leaders.

Part of the risk in the entrepreneurial attitude is that by always generating changes and improvements, it creates confusion and instability in the organization. The entrepreneur's search for innovation challenges the established processes and with that, those who execute them. His enthusiasm is such that, in order to keep the project going, he resorts to encouraging, intimidating, praising, flattering, yelling and promising anything. He cannot surrender to the discouragement of others or due to obstacles or adversities. He is an engine that is constantly running.

For his part, the role of **manager** is pragmatic. Without the manager, there would be no planning, order and predictability. This is the perspective or personality that is responsible for ensuring that the company has plastic boxes where the screws, nuts and other elements will be stored. If it is a workshop, they will have a wall board with the tools drawn on it to keep them tidy and available. Everything in its place.

If the entrepreneur lives in the future, the manager lives in the past. While the entrepreneur seeks to have control, the manager longs to establish order. He studies information about what has happened in order to establish control measures. For him, events and changes are nothing but problems to be solved, inconveniences. However, just as without the entrepreneurial attitude we would not have improvements, without the participation of the managerial attitude the business would not survive, or it would be extremely unstable.

The third of the roles to be executed to achieve the company's success is that of the **technician**. He is a doer. His creed can be summed up in the phrase, "If you want it done, do it yourself." He loves to carry out objectives. For him, thinking is an unproductive activity. He is not interested in ideas, but in how to execute them. He does not like changes, nor the unknown. The technician's perspective is to live in the present. He is an individualist, since he sees everything from the perspective of doing it himself. When the manager wants to order his processes, establish controls and other administrative actions, the technician considers him a meddler who only complicates his functions.

It is difficult to find those three elements in one person. When someone covers all three roles, they reach a very high and balanced level of competence. If we don't have the skills to perform this trio of fundamental components, it is convenient to team up with whoever complements us; but it is essential that all three exist in our company. By doing so, we will have a solid and balanced organization. We will have an entrepreneur who provides innovative ideas, products and services, a manager who establishes the order and methods necessary to manage resources and fulfill promises to the clients, and a technician who can operate the processes and, in that way, we will rely on the magic of the number three.

Earlier, I mentioned that in addition to the three basic roles necessary for a company to succeed, you need three points of support that every entrepreneur must possess. These are: ***mind, heart and education***. The mind or intellect is where the theoretical perspectives that provide direction to the company are developed. It is where they enrich the vision, mission, focus, objectives, plans and strategies. From the heart comes the passion and motivation that give us the impetus to start the company and keep fighting against all odds. This enthusiasm incites the mind to generate a firm commitment; it produces the determination that allows the organization to survive despite the difficulties.

The mind and the heart are like open legs when we stand

on the boat, and our third point of support, equivalent to one of the arms, is education. Now more than ever, we need to be updated and informed to thrive in business. An entrepreneur must constantly learn about their market, finances, strategy, human relations, communication and other basic elements of business and human development. Remember that business is done between people; for this reason, it is essential to acquire skills to deal with people, to create new relationships and to ensure the solidity of those we already have.

This is what I discovered when I took the Dale Carnegie Method of Human Relations seminar. From that moment, I understood that human development is not only something that helps us to live better, but it also provides us with knowledge and tools to be more competent.

Our network marketing business has a powerful education system, which is what makes it highly effective. With this method, we maintain ourselves in a constant dynamic of reading, listening to speakers and learning about the various factors that make companies and leaders prosper. Another great advantage is that, by operating as a team, you have other people who complement those functions in which you are not very good, and you have the opportunity to support them in the ones where you perform best. Our companies are designed so that, like a tripod, you have the support points you need to thrive. Having this variety of complementary backups and business roles increases the likelihood that our project will prosper and prevents us from becoming part of the regrettable statistic of the failures that befall many entrepreneurs.

Owing to the fact that I learned this, I now have the resources and the time to carry out this wonderful voyage across the Atlantic Ocean. Applying these principles has given me the freedom to have enough fishing rods and, therefore, many fish.

I invite you to reflect on this. **Do you have enough hooks in the water?** Do you depend on the income of a job? Have you considered the alternative of starting your own business? Do you think you have the profile to execute the three roles required of the business man or woman? Is there a business project in your mind and heart? Have you researched network marketing companies as an alternative in order to start fishing seriously? Do you know someone who is doing it? Aren't you worried that one day your only water tap might be shut off? Remember, the greater the number of lines in the water, the greater the chance that you'll increase your catch.

Speaking of aquatic animals and returning to our voyage, today we experienced an extraordinary moment. While we were plying the sea, we passed through an area where several flying fish glided around our boat. They jumped and floated in the same direction, resembling a synchronized swimming choreography. It is a spectacle to see them emerge from the water and fly through the air. They spread their wings like birds do to fly a certain distance and then dive into the sea again.

This is one of the sights that you can only experience offshore. To our surprise and enjoyment, some of these aerodynamic animals fell on the deck. By taking them and observing their bodies closely, we could see their thin, brilliant skin change color. Because of their shape, they looked like small metallic torpedoes with semitransparent wings. They looked so energetic. Having them aboard the catamaran was a waste. We didn't want to see them perish among us and they aren't the kind of fish we would eat. For that reason, what we did with these unexpected crew members of *El Impulso* was to return them to their habitat, but not before bidding them farewell and thanking them for visiting us.

In the air, their bodies shone as they reflected the sun's rays. The school floated about and sank back into the water. The dance continued for several minutes. They seemed to be heading in the same direction as us. I didn't know if their destination would also be in the Caribbean, but they pushed on ahead like us, where beyond the horizon, Martinique Island continued to wait for us.

THREE FUNDAMENTAL FACTORS

19th Nautical Day 11.28.2016

On this day, my watch started again at 00:00 and I finished it at 03:00. We sailed at 1.5 knots with the mainsail and calm seas. We changed course 180° to the south to catch the slight wind of three knots that blew there. With this move, we managed to catch it from the port side and we got the code zero out. Thus, we increased our speed a little to 3.5 knots.

At 02:00 hours, we rolled up the code zero and continued sailing with the mainsail at 1.5 knots.

Today the wind is so light that our advance is very slow. It is in these moments of calm when the sea teaches you and reminds you that you must be patient. Sailing is a very uncomfortable experience for those who don't take calm times calmly. Dear sailors, when circumstances don't work in your favor, it is necessary to maintain confidence in oneself and not allow even a hint of doubt about not reaching your destination. Even though the sea is calm, and the wind is asleep, I know we will arrive in Martinique. Maybe it won't be when we had planned, but we will get there.

If things are not going as you wish, do not get exasperated. Hopelessness only adds another factor against you, and leads you to make thoughtless decisions. When we act with despair, we usually make bad decisions. It is very valuable to learn to move to the rhythm of nature; in this case, to the rhythm of the wind and the ocean. To fight against them is like betting to lose, because the natural processes do not know about haste or slowness. We are the ones who live with watches on our wrists and calculating everything based on time. We have become slaves to schedules and haste. The sea knows nothing about times, schedules and calendars. Therefore, the best thing is to learn to move at its pace and enjoy the journey while you do it.

Our geographical location at 11:12 was latitude 21° 19′ north and longitude 50° 05′ west with a heading of 253°. This course is the one that takes us directly to the island of Martinique, straight to the finish line. For bad weather, have a good breakfast. Today for lunch we had toast with oil and tomato, some slices of chorizo and Manchego cheese, as well as a cookie with chocolate. In addition to this drink, we had apple juice and milk. At 11:30 am, we did our physical exercises: *"Gym tonic"* to exercise the body and mind, as well as a few Pilates.

Throughout the journey, we took time to exercise. It is essential for our bodies to remain nimble and awake. In addition, exercising with others is easier than doing so alone. In my case, I tried to exercise even when others didn't want to. I have learned that neglecting the body is a big mistake that you end up regretting.

During the trip, we have developed good relations between the crew. This has helped us a lot to ensure that the voyage is pleasant and enjoyable. When there are problems among the members of a crew, the situations become extremely uncomfortable. Also, aboard a boat, you have no alternative; you are going to remain inside it surrounded by the same people, who you need and who need you to face adversities and reach the destination.

Fortunately, we have had a good time together. We have managed to live together in peace and with camaraderie. We divide up our tasks, we have fun times, we exercise, we support each other by manning our watches; we have good gatherings and we also respect each other's private times.

Enjoy the trip

Today I want to invite you not to forget some simple, but important factors that make your adventure more bearable and fruitful. The first is to take care of your relationships with the rest of the sailors that board your boat or cross your path. **Dealing with others is essential to have a full life.** As human beings, we live our lives focused on having, achieving and hoarding, only to realize at the end of the trip that the most valuable thing was to enjoy the people who accompanied us. Material goods, although important, are not the purpose of life. The people are the most important. I doubt that anyone regrets, in the twilight of their years, not having acquired a better car or bought a ring with more carats. What we regret is not having spent more time with our children, not hugging our grandchildren, not sharing our dreams with our spouse with an espresso in our hand; not thanking our parents; not talking with siblings and sharing with friends a good bottle of wine, tapas, snacks and a lot of laughter.

To wander through life without stopping to enjoy being with the people around us more is a waste. I congratulate myself for the multitude of friends I have. I consider myself privileged to know that in several latitudes and different meridians, we have friends whom we love very much and with whom we have spent spectacular times. But this does not happen by chance; it requires spending time, planning, investing time and finding them. The same applies to the family. On many occasions, we take for granted that the people we value—and even ourselves—will be there forever.

Dear sailors: Make no mistake, it is our encounters with others that enrich our days. The path of existence is very short to waste in resentment, discomfort and silence. Let's make peace with the sailors and enjoy the time we spend together.

Another point that I want to emphasize and that I

mentioned briefly before, is the importance of enjoying the journey. Success is not only about reaching the goal, but actually enjoying the process that takes you there. In our adventure across the ocean, this truth is more than evident. Every morning, we enjoy the air and the view. We are happy when the marine life greets us and passes around the boat. We have fun when we share food or when we fish. We have taken time to bathe in the ocean and to lay ourselves down on the deck to sunbathe. Although the destination is Martinique, the enjoyment of the journey is an integral part of the intellectual, mental and spiritual nourishment.

In the same way, we should turn this into a habit of life and of course, work. If we think that the only satisfactory thing is payday or receiving an important salary, we will stop enjoying the rest of the days. In our network marketing company, we live with many friends; we help others to develop; we meet people constantly and visit cities to share with people the opportunity to become independent and prosper. People don't always accept our proposal, but it doesn't matter; that is also part of the growth. The rejections of some edify us and add value to the fact that there are those who accept our proposal to take up this career, in favor of their financial and personal freedom.

Dear sailor on the voyage of existence, do not miss the chance to enjoy every step along the way. Remember that *it is precisely on the road where things happen.* What good is it to be in a beautiful catamaran if you don't enjoy the air that rushes past your face? What is the benefit of crossing the Atlantic if you do not share the moment and have fun with your companions in adventure? Why despair to get to the destination if there is so much beauty in the journey? When we only focus on how much is left before reaching Martinique, we stop appreciating the dolphins, the birds that perch on the mast, the stars that flood the sky at night and so many other things that you can only see during the voyage.

Time for you

The last piece of advice that I would like to share with you is that from time to time, you take some time to reflect, to undergo a catharsis, as the Greeks used to do to purify themselves and get rid of the negative things that kept them from moving forward. Today, meditation or mindfulness is done, which helps us control our mind. How important it is to have those moments with yourself! In everyday life, **we have forgotten to be with ourselves**. We come, we go, we get up, we eat, we work, we meet, we run, we walk, we take public transport, we go to the store, we go to the cinema and we fall down into our beds exhausted, to give our body time to recover, because the next day it will be the same—and the next and the next will be the same. In the midst of so much bustle, we forget to stop and think. Let's take a few minutes to analyze our actions, plan our day, review what really matters and find our priorities.

At sea, you have that opportunity. The absence of noise and everyday activities becomes a blessing. The presence of water and sky, instead of buildings, traffic lights, streets and the huge outdoor advertising billboards, gives you a peaceful framework that, little by little, reduces the intensity that we had before boarding *El Impulso*.

In these peaceful times, I wonder if I will recover them when I'm back in Madrid. My intention is to do so, because when I take the time to reconsider, things begin to fall into place and what really matters emerges. To recover what's really valuable, it is essential to stop, shut down the locomotive of daily routine and sit down to examine our actions and priorities. Only through self-analysis will we discover how far we are from the course we wish to take. This way, we will take our compass and our navigational charts to correct any deviation. I invite you to schedule these moments to meet with yourself.

I know, dear sailors, that many of you will not make this journey; that your sea is the city or maybe the countryside. That's fine. Not everyone has sailor's blood. However, that doesn't stop you from being a sailor. In your journey, you face great waves that test your character; you live with limited resources, like us aboard the sailboat; it rains at night and sometimes, the water starts to pour into the bilge of your family or your economy. Your own sea poses daily challenges and you will have to face them calmly and wisely, leaning on other crew members and having a clear idea of your port of destination. We all sail along the journey of life.

The sea continues to be still. The advance has been slow. However, today we had a spectacular meal. We started with cold pasta and salad, followed by a chicken breast and as the main dish, an exquisite Asturian stew, which, although it was canned, we enjoyed joyfully. As if this were not enough, our dessert was nougat ice cream. Faced with such plentiful food and because I did not have to stand watch, I took a comforting nap. Since the wind was still absent, we sailed by motor with a speed of six knots. At 18:00 hours, the force of the wind increased to ten knots. We unfurled the code zero, which together with the mainsail, gave us more speed. We reduced the engine speed and decided to turn it off at 18:30. We continue sailing with a speed of five knots.

You are an adventurer, a man or a woman with longings and abilities. Do not stop your boat; dare to venture out into your ocean.

LESSONS OF CHARACTER AND HUMILITY

21st Nautical Day 11.30.2016

Today I started a new watch schedule, from 03:00 to 06:00. Yesterday was my last shift from 00:00 to 03:00 hours. During the watches, the responsibility of the ship is in your hands. It is a very serious commitment, as the rest of the crew are trusting their lives to whoever is on watch. This is the reason why you cannot be a successful crew member if you lack the character to take on this level of obligation. What I find very positive is that, knowing your travel companions, you don't doubt their integrity to take care of the boat. This is something that I learned throughout my professional career. You have to trust your collaborators and they have to trust you. If we each do our part, everything will go well. If one of the sailors does not behave with integrity, the entire crew is in danger.

Of course, this doesn't just happen on boats. It happens

in any organization and even in our personal relationships. When a person defrauds the trust of others, the domino effect occurs. Companies require a team of committed and upright partners. *If you cannot trust your people, you wear yourself out supervising them*, writing reports and carrying out other control activities. On the other hand, when people have gained the trust of others with their actions, you know that they will back you, that they are with you and that they also have the certainty that you will do the same.

Professional and personal ethics

I remember that in one of my engineering jobs, I was responsible for acquiring machinery for a very large project. It was not just any negotiation; that purchase meant a lot of money. Therefore, it was important to choose the best option, both in performance and price. I inquired with different suppliers and brands to find the best option.

During the process, one of the suppliers invited me to dinner to talk about the project. Sitting at the table was the owner of his company. We started the conversation with the usual protocols, chatting about generalities, sports and hobbies. The owner of this company told me that he knew I liked to sail. He knew about my love for the sea and my desire to acquire a sailboat at some point in my life. I nodded and replied that this was one of my dreams.

We chatted for a few minutes about the marvelous world

of the sea, boats, ports to visit and other details of the sea. Suddenly, with a smiling look and trying to work the following proposal into our current conversation, he told me that if I bought the machinery from them, my dream would come true, because they would give me a sailboat. At that very moment, I got up from the table, I said goodbye and I never welcomed them back in my office. An entire company was trusting in me to make the best choice. My decision would affect the production of a plant and the company's results for years, and **a personal benefit can never be the best alternative when dealing with a decision for the team.** A sailor on watch cannot afford any concessions. Things must be done correctly. The others are trusting that while you're on duty, everything will be fine. I am a faithful believer that we must strive to achieve our goals, but we must do it properly and, above all, in an upright manner. The shortcuts that betray others and our own values never lead to a good port.

God and life reward our actions. Years later, and thanks to the fruits of my network marketing business, I acquired a sailboat and was able to navigate the European coasts without having a single regret and proud to know that I had earned, with my work, the right to own *Libertad 1*.

We require that same level of integrity to do business and to watch over the boat while our shipmates sleep. They rest confident that the lookout will do his work, without a single deviation. During the watches, you must be wide awake and watchful over the course and surroundings. *No sailor will prosper if he does not know how to act*

with diligence. When you are on watch, you must take full responsibility and for that, you must be willing to do what you need to do and have the knowledge to do it.

Having this level of character implies, in addition to maintaining your integrity, performing tasks that without a degree of maturity you would consider insignificant or unworthy. You have to take care of every detail and do everything that's at hand and is your responsibility. There are even activities that we do not consider part of our obligations, and we can do them without investing a lot of time, increasing the effectiveness of the team.

Humility opens roads

A good lesson I learned about this happened during my stay in Matsuyama, Japan. My job there was to train a team of 24 Spanish engineers and, together with them, learn how the factory works, and then set up a similar one in Spain. In the factory, I had a private space, "the office of the project director." It seemed wonderful to me that, at my 29 years of age, I had already reached that level at work.

In the first two days, I noticed something that seemed strange to me. When the day ended, and I left the office, I noticed that the janitor had left a bucket and mop right outside my door. That carelessness did not match how careful and orderly the Japanese were in every detail.

On the third day, when I left the office, I saw that the

cleaning utensils were again there. I didn't wait any longer and I told one of my Japanese colleagues that the janitor was leaving his work tools outside my area. He kindly explained that he put them there so that I could clean my office before going home. It was part of my responsibilities and that of any coworker in regard to their own space. It was a quicker and easier way to do it.

That day I learned that in their culture, **your status or position do not exempt you from the work you can** do to collaborate, regardless of whether you think it is beneath your level or not. When you realize this, you find other activities in which you can contribute. Pride is a hindrance to effectiveness. It only took a few minutes for the "project manager" to dip the mop in the bucket and wipe the floor before the end of the day. With this action, I obtained two things of great importance and value: I had a clean office and a little more humility. That day, I not only started to wash the floor of my office, but also to purify some corners of my soul.

The same must be done in our project. There are activities that we consider more valuable than others, but we must do them all. If we believe that some of the tasks are for positions of another level, we are not acting with a team perspective, but from the traditional proud position of the big boss. In *El Impulso*, all the crew members had to do all kinds of tasks, from standing watch to washing dishes and toilets. None of these tasks is degrading; they are all necessary to have clean spaces, prepared foods, available tools and to work better during the voyage.

What activities do you have in your job that you could do, without waiting for someone else to do them? Are you taking on the role of a boss and forgetting that of a collaborator? If you're a man, do you participate in housework or do you just let your partner do it? We do not need to be Japanese to apply this lesson of humility and solidarity.

Yesterday, the handle for the spinnaker broke and we were left without this sail, which is what allows us to increase speed when the winds are low. We set about to repair it, but as an immediate solution, we took out the mainsail and opened the genoa to starboard, with good winds from the stern. As for our route, we have 547 nautical miles left to reach our destination. According to the plan made at the beginning and the experiences of other sailors who made this trip, we should have arrived in Martinique yesterday. Since we have had several days with very little wind, we are not moving according to our schedule. This delay means that it will take us twenty-five percent more time than what we had planned.

When you are in such a situation, you are grateful that, throughout the journey, you've fed on what you fished and that each day, we rationed the water and what we had for food. In fact, we caught three mahi-mahi this morning and we caught three more in the afternoon. Forethought is an act of prudence that allows you to protect yourself from unexpected situations. The important thing was that, despite knowing about our delay, we did not desist or get frustrated, but instead kept moving forward with joy, because the important thing is that we were convinced we would arrive. As mariners, we understand that we do not modify the navigational plan or the route. The plans were altered by circumstances beyond our control. And as the saying goes: "Look on the bright side."

Do what you have to do

Determination is the key to not giving up. During the conferences and consulting work that I provide for our businesses' partners, I share with them that this feature is the most important for growth. Determination is a state of consciousness or, more profoundly, of the spirit, where there is no point of return. Dear sailor, I want to share with you an adventure that I had a few years ago, related to determination. This happened during my visit to the nation of Mauritius, to the east of southern Africa. This land is a beautiful and small island country of extraordinary landscapes. One day, I got away to climb its well-known "mountain of lakes." At the top, I found a large spring of fresh water which lead to a waterfall that emptied into seven other lakes. From there, you could rappel down into the middle of the waterfall. I had never practiced that sport and the height of the place was about fifty meters, the equivalent of a fifteen-story building.

When I peeked over the edge and looked at the next

lake, a chill ran through my entire body. The risk was great and my experience non-existent. However, I decided that since I was up there, I would not go down the same way I had climbed up. They put the harness on me, and I got on the rope and started down toward the lake. The water in the waterfall bathed me, the rocks were slippery and the distance to *terra firma* seemed endless. After a great effort and sticking to the advice they gave me before going down, I managed to get down to the lake.

It is determination that makes you achieve what you propose. When you decide to invest your life in a project, you must continue until you finish it. There is no way back. Never give up, that's my motto.

If you currently find yourself where I was, on the top of the mountain, and the view down below makes you afraid, do not give up. Maybe you are going through a time when your project, your relationship, your family or your business are in a crisis. I invite you to obtain the determination to save them, to fight for what you long for and not give up. You may not be arriving at your destination at the scheduled time or under the circumstances you planned. In any case, do not give up, **and allow your sailor spirit to take control.** Do not pay attention to the height of the mountain, the cloudy sky or the negative forecasts of the press or other people. The sailor stands in the middle of the storm, convinced that the rainstorm will pass and that after it's gone, if he keeps sailing, the destination port will appear.

The reality that I learned in the journey of my life, is that, *if you want to advance, prosper and break out of your routine, you will have to dare and risk.* This means taking the "leap" to cut loose the mooring lines and get out of that comfort zone called complacency that keeps us tied to our port. To overcome that state that does not allow us to change our lives, we must take the leap that frees us from routine and settling for the ordinary. I know that this is not easy and that it requires determination or someone else who challenges you to draw out that gift and value that lives within you. To document the above, let me tell you this anecdote that made me take another leap in my life.

One of the pastimes we have in my family is spending Christmas skiing somewhere in the world. It was December 31, 2016, and my entire family, thirteen in all, was enjoying a gala dinner to say goodbye to the year at the Club Med ski resort in France, very close to Montblanc. During this celebration and with that festive atmosphere, my eldest son came over to me to toast and said, "Dad, what do you say we go paragliding tomorrow when we go up to ski?" I looked at him with some skepticism because I thought he was teasing me and, with a sarcastic smile, I replied, "Of course. Tomorrow we jump."

The next morning, just as we were starting the new year climbing the chairlift, my son says to me, "Dad, the paragliding trainers are already there waiting for us on the platform at three thousand meters to make the jump." I turned my face to him and with great excitement

I said, "But weren't you joking last night?!" "No, Dad, I was serious," to which I replied, "Are you all right in the head? We have never gone paragliding." And he replied, "That's why, dad, we'll have to experience it sometime. And you've always told me that in life, you have to dare and jump." At that moment, I kept silent and I had no option but accepting the challenge so as to be consistent with my teaching.

We arrived at the platform and saw there were the two coaches waiting for us with their paragliders. They explained what we were going to do and how we should behave. The objective was to place ourselves on the platform with the skis and let ourselves fall down a slope of about 500 meters, at the end of which there were a lot of stones and trees. The instructor tied himself to me and adjusted the paraglider to our back, and when we were on the edge of the slope, he whispered in my ear, "Miguel, are you ready? Well then, jump!"

We started descending down the slope with increasing speed! My heart was beating a thousand times an hour and adrenaline flowed through my being at great speed. I saw how the stones and the trees grew bigger and bigger. Suddenly, I felt a strong pull backward and saw the skis lose contact with the earth. We began to rise above the stones and trees. What a wonderful and exciting feeling! We climbed to a height of more than 3,500 meters, from where, like the eye of the eagle, we took in all the beauty that nature offers us from the sky.

We flew over mountains, forests, glaciers and enjoyed

watching the deer running through the virgin snow. In short, it was a show that I could never forget and a wonderful and exciting feeling that is still alive in me. There was a price to pay, yes! I had to overcome fear, of course; but the prize was so great that I will never forget this new leap in my life. Do not forget that *life, from the moment we're born until we leave, is about daring, risking and jumping;* the rest is routine and boredom.

The binoculars of the mind

Today, while I was at the bow of the ship, I thought I saw something strange in the distance floating in the water. I quickly grabbed the binoculars to see more clearly what I had seen on the surface of the ocean. In my haste to discover it, I held the binoculars backwards. As a result, my target was so far away that I could not see anything. I reacted and turned the binoculars around, focused on the object and to my surprise, saw a huge whale coming toward us. My curiosity was so great, that I zoomed in to bring its image closer. Thanks to the effect of the lens, it looked like I had that beautiful animal by my side. I could make out his eyes, his whiskers and other details of his body. Having used the binoculars in the right way made all the difference. It was wonderful.

In the afternoon, in my time of relaxation and rest, I thought about the binoculars and the whale mentioned above. I realized why many people do not move forward in life, do not overcome and do not realize their dreams. And I would like to share with you these reflections, because if you are in a situation of stagnation, without moving forward, living in routine, in fatigue and unmotivated by more of the same, I will explain what may be the cause of that and how you can change the situation. Believe me, everything depends on the view or outlook of your mind. I will show it with a drawing to explain it more easily. This is a way of looking at things used by many people who achieved what they wanted for their lives, and like us, have applied successfully.

HOW PEOPLE SEE THE FUTURE

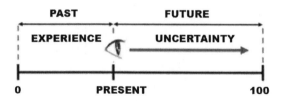

Figure 1

Look at figure 1 and imagine that it represents the life cycle of any human being. Divide it into three parts: when you are born (point "0"), the present and when you pass away (point "100"). As you will observe in the drawing, the mental outlook of what you want to do, achieve, undertake, etc., goes from the present to the future. By doing so, you will always find many obstacles that can make you quit.

The reason for this is the following: We will call the time that's elapsed from the moment you were born until the present the experience of life; that is, everything that has happened to you, whether good or bad.

This is filed in your subconscious. If your last years have not been positive, but on the contrary have been hard, with serious problems, disappointments, etc., then your recent experiences will be negative. Thus, starting from that present and with a negative perspective, you will visualize your future. Your perception will be conditioned by those last experiences and your vision will be pessimistic. You will be looking out with the binoculars of your mind pointed backwards. You will see a future of uncertainty, as if you were in a dark tunnel where you cannot see the light at the end of it. This way of seeing produces fears that, in general, stop human beings from taking the leap that will take them out of their routine and comfort zone. When we hold the binoculars of the mind backwards, we use phrases like the following that denote nothing but acquiescence and fear: "Better the devil you know than the one you don't know."

But there is another way of looking at it, and it is by using the binoculars correctly. This will allow you to have a clear and up-close image of the future. This way of observing the future will project your vision in an adequate way to achieve what you most desire in life. If you truly have dreams or goals that you want to achieve in five, ten or fifty years, trust in me and let's play a little mental game. I want you to imagine that we are sitting in the DeLorean car from the movie *Back to the Future*.

We are no longer going to see things from the present that keeps us tied to the problems of the past.

We are inside this powerful car that, without any trouble, will take us to the ideal future. We will go mentally to the year in which you want to fulfill your goals. ***Imagine yourself in that future that you ardently desire.*** See your wishes fulfilled and recreate them so intensely in your mind and heart until it seems to you that you have already achieved them. You are already where you wanted to be, you already have what you wanted to have. Awaken the emotions produced by your victory, by your success. See yourself sharing your achievements with your friends and family. Your emotions and enthusiasm are barely contained; it is as if right now you were touching those fulfilled wishes with your hands. Close your eyes and carry out the visualization exercise as accurately and specifically as possible.

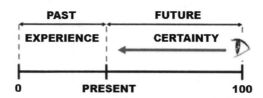

HOW WE SHOULD SEE IT

> WITH REGARD TO EVERYTHING THAT EXISTS IN THIS LIFE, THERE WAS ALWAYS SOMEONE WHO FIRST SAW IT AND LIVED IT IN THEIR MIND, AND THEN MADE IT A REALITY.

Figure 2

Did you see it? Did you go to your future? Did you feel that wonderful sensation that reaching our goals produces? What happened is that you went to the future where your dreams came true. And it is from there, with that belief, that you must look at your present, as shown in figure 2. From that ideal future, optimistic and motivating, you realize that you have already mentally traveled the path you must take. With that certainty that you can achieve it and having visualized your future, you will be determined that your goals will become reality.

Summing up the above, all desires can be achieved, but we must see them with the binoculars of the mind in their correct position, starting from the future we want, and not from our negative and difficult past. I invite you to perform the visualization exercise again. ***Dare to imagine that ideal future in which your goals are already in your hands.*** Take the list of your dreams so that, as clearly as possible, you can see them with the eyes of your imagination. Do it, catch them with the binoculars of your mind and, once you have them with you, from there, from that perfect future, start the path toward them. Remember that history has taught us that everything that has been created in this life was due to the fact that the creator dared to transport himself mentally to the future to make those dreams come true.

The beautiful creature that I spotted with the binoculars approached our boat. It came so close that I no longer needed the binoculars to observe it. It had turned into something close, clear and real. It positioned itself next to the catamaran and stayed there for a good while. Its length exceeded our boat and who knows what its weight was. It was immense in size, about twenty meters long. Our ship looked small and fragile beside it. Nevertheless, as much in me as in the rest of the crew, the sensation that was produced in us was not one of fear, but of admiration, enthusiasm and gratitude.

It greeted us by expelling hot air from its body, which condensed like a great stream of water upon coming into contact with the outside. Those details of its body which I could only observe through the binoculars were now visible to the naked eye. Seeing this sea Goliath was a real spectacle, a great gift from the ocean and its inhabitants; an experience that you can only experience by being a sailor. It continued beside us for a few more minutes to wish us a good afternoon and remind us that in the ocean, as in life, we are never alone.

LAND AHOY!

24th Nautical Day 12.3.2016

Our position at 12:00 hours is latitude 15° 04′ north and longitude 59° 52′, heading 249°. Today is the big day. We are scheduled to arrive at the port of Martinique around 23:30. On this day, I'm overcome with emotion and my thoughts grow in strength and rise to the surface; yet in spite of being so close to our goal, we have had to fulfill our daily tasks. With the emotion contained within my chest, I did my last load of laundry, exercised for half an hour and took time to read. This practice is one of my habits that I consider a virtue. I had not written in previous journal entries that throughout the tour, I was able to read several books.

For me, **constant reading is key to having an agile mind and updated knowledge.** I am convinced that one of the best ways to keep learning is through reading. Since I discovered the importance of post-university training, by attending workshops, courses and conferences; I also understood the importance of being a good reader. This habit was consolidated when I started our business together with my wife, and since then, I continue to practice it. I consider it one of the central reasons for the successes that I have achieved.

Back to the narrative of the day, today it was my turn to wash the dishes. By the way, our menu for the day was one of luxury. The meal featured mussels and razor clams as an appetizer. The main dish was chickpeas sautéed with tomato and onion and pan-cooked tuna. The dessert consisted of chocolate nougat and a glass of red wine.

Yesterday at 17:30, we had a beautiful farewell by a group of young dolphins. It was about 10:00 when they joined our boat, with their aerodynamic bodies moving at full speed. They played among themselves, with the sailboat and with us. They seemed to know that we were about to finish a long, risky and wonderful voyage and they gave us a matchless "grand finale." Observing these wonderful mammals in their natural environment is a spectacle without equal. I could feel the miracle of life and the powerful bond between all the creatures of the planet. I became one with the whole.

The graceful cetaceans jumped and, like a perfect synchronized swimming team, crossed from the bow to the stern and then repeated the feat in the opposite direction. At times, showing off their great ability, they placed themselves between the skids of the catamaran without touching them, despite the fact that we had good speed. They jumped, mingled among themselves, disappeared for seconds and then they would show themselves in a wonderful water display. When we could no longer see them, they would force us to turn around on the ship to see where they would appear. They kept this up for just under an hour and then vanished to the bottom, to their home that we would soon abandon to return to our innate habitat, dry land.

During dinner, it was inevitable that we would comment on the dolphins and the other animal sightings we had witnessed. We remember the several whales that had visited us, the flying fish that came on board and of course, the wonderful nocturnal performance of the fluorescent plankton and the stars. Images and moments that we will never forget. Eternal memories of our journey across the Atlantic.

With this trip, I confirmed something that has always been inside me, but became evident during the journey: *Being in contact with nature energizes us and elevates the spirit*. We need to surround ourselves with a natural environment in order not to lose our essence and open our minds to what is really valuable. Thinking like this reminds us that *the most beautiful and significant things are not obtained with money*.

Today, to continue with the shows offered by the sea for free, I could not miss the dawn. Even though I did not have an early watch assigned, I got up early to watch the sunrise. While on deck, the air penetrated my lungs, filling them with a sense of indescribable purity. The sea breeze drew trails of moisture upon my skin, and the sun, still warm and soft, began to cast its rays without even showing itself on the horizon.

Be thankful

When facing so much beauty, it is impossible not to thank God for life and for the wonderful designs He created for our delight. As for gratefulness, this day was a special one, with double or triple gratitude, because besides the spectacular times at sea, it fulfilled another of my dreams. As if that wasn't enough, in the afternoon I also watched the setting of the king of the stars, with its impressive metamorphosis of colors, but with a different perspective now, knowing that it was the last sunset of the crossing. The light turned a shade of ochre after having passed through shades of violet, pink and lastly, different intensities of orange.

I was facing a beautiful sunset, at the end of a great odyssey and in the sunset of my life. Age has given me the wrinkles that emerged years ago in my skin, mainly on my face, neck and arms; but **old age appears when you allow the folds and roughness to grow in your soul.** My spirit and my attitude are strong and eager for new goals that I intend to achieve. I know young people who have allowed their hearts to be full of wrinkles. On the outside, the body indicates a certain age, but their attitude reveals an old soul. They live without hope and without desires; they have become accustomed to the routine that life presented to them, and they have forgotten that they have the power to modify it. They have believed the social lies of "This is the life I was dealt," "It's impossible," "You can't do it," and they grew old very early.

The wonderful thing about our inner being is that it can be rejuvenated whenever we decide. This is a great gift that we have. We can relive life and diminish our inner age with a positive and dreaming attitude. The youth of the soul returns when we choose to recover our entrepreneurial spirit, the spirit of sailors. If this is your case, I urge you to stop seeing the circumstances and focus on what you can do to get out of them. Maybe you cannot change them, but you can modify your way of dealing with them. You are not destined to die in the place where you were born—you can get out of there. You also do not have to spend all your life in the same job. You are not required to have had schooling to be an entrepreneur, nor does your family life have to be the way you don't like it. Everything can be transformed, we can all change. Any of us has the potential to improve our situation. It is a matter of deciding, making up our minds, and acting. And of course, **age is not an impediment.**

Faced with our imminent arrival to terra firma, the feeling is wonderful and contradictory. On the one hand, I am close to wrapping up an almost month-long voyage across the Atlantic on a sailboat from Spain to America. This means achieving one of the dreams that was simmering in my mind for many, many years. The satisfaction of fulfilling it is extraordinary and it confirms, once again, that *it is determination converted into action that leads us to reach our goals.* However, on the inside, there is a part of me that does not want to conclude this trip. It has been such a rewarding experience and its blessings have been so numerous that I'm pained to see it end. This experience has given me a very profound and clarifying lesson. In the solitude of the sea, I found many answers to a multitude of questions that nested in my mind. It has been a trip to the deepest part of my being, where I found solutions to what seemed like obstacles, but I discovered that they were simply fears that we create in our imagination. I have concluded that the reason people do not succeed is because they make excuses or because they accept adversity as reasons for giving up.

Throughout the days of the voyage, I have lived magical moments that have made me understand that **life is meant to be enjoyed and meant for us to be happy.** But the greatest thing is that all of us, those of us with the spirit of sailors and entrepreneurs, have the same possibilities to achieve our dreams. This is not a privilege for a few, but an invitation for anyone willing to take the necessary actions to achieve it. That is why, dear sailors, I have decided to share my trip with you. It is my purpose to motivate people to revive their dreams and remember that with determination they will be able to achieve them. In addition, I have taken the opportunity to share some of the reflections and learnings I have had, not only in this odyssey, but also throughout the longest voyage, that of life itself.

Maybe your longings have nothing to do with the sea, but I am sure that within you there are several or perhaps many dreams to fulfill. Do not give up, do not let them die, do not go to the grave with them inside your heart. Work to achieve them, strive, share them with your loved ones, start giving them existence with your mouth. Allow them to leave your mind and turn them into written plans and talks with your friends and loved ones. Dreams are built with those kinds of actions. Give them the opportunity to live and enrich your existence.

This yearning of mine has lasted more than three weeks. It has been twenty-four extraordinary days. Seven men isolated ourselves from our routines, jobs, businesses and families to meet our goal: to cross the Atlantic Ocean on a sailboat. If you knew each of us, you would see that we are very different, in age, professions and our beliefs. However, we have something in common that united us and provided us with the camaraderie, respect and teamwork to realize this odyssey: the same dream.

The Caribbean sky bid farewell to the day, but it welcomed us clothed in multiple colors and with the freshness of the evening air. We were close to urban life, but still totally surrounded by water and sky. The day was just hours from ending and with it, the conclusion of our adventure was also approaching. The stars had not appeared yet; maybe Mars had already showed its brilliance—I do not know. I did not check to see. But what I did see was a slight blue figure in the distance that spontaneously unleashed in my throat the repeated shouting of the phrase:

LAND AHOY!

The Voyage

Epilogue

D ear reader, we have reached the end of the voyage. After 24 days of sailing together, I would like to thank you for having shared this incredible trip with me, in which we not only crossed the Atlantic, but also shared an important part of the journey of my life.

I deeply hope that you have enjoyed it and that my life experiences help and inspire you, so that you can also sail your seas and reach the desired port of your dreams.

If you have not yet decided to leave behind the port of routine and settling for the ordinary, you just have to remember that the key to casting off is: DARE, RISK AND MAKE THE LEAP. I can assure you that if you do, your life will change drastically, and you will know a very different dimension, where only the "mentality of abundance and prosperity" will live in each of my dear readers.

Whether you cast off or if you continue to dock at the port, I invite you to contact me, with any question or query, via my social network pages:

Email: latravesia@aglobal.es
Twitter: www.twitter.com/miguelaguado

Thanks

To the Amway Corporation for its values: Freedom, Hope, Family and Rewards, by providing me with the vehicle to achieve my freedom, that of my family and that of thousands of people whom I have influenced so that they also achieved it.

To all the members of the *El Impulso* crew: Enrique Sebastian, Enry, Mario, Antonio 1, Antonio 2 and Carlos, because without them the journey would not have been as fun.

To my great friend Juan, since he was the one who encouraged me to write a book several years ago, to share my personal, professional and business experiences with the world.

To all human beings with an entrepreneurial and overcoming spirit, because they are the ones who leave behind legacies in their passage through this world and who become our inspiration.

About the Author

Miguel Aguado was born in Madrid, Spain. He studied Nautical Sciences, a branch of engineering, and since finishing his degree at the age of 22, he has worked in various fields, including the naval engineering, petrochemical, textile chemistry and automotive industries.

During 25 years of professional life, he completed hundreds of technical courses and a very special one in Human Relations, led by Dale Carnegie in 1976, which marked his life and career. His greatest professional aspirations culminated in 1980, when he was hired as Director of Engineering by General Motors Components of Spain, with a subsequent promotion to Research and Development and Plant Superintendent.

By the end of 1988, he made the decision to change the direction of his life and created his network marketing company, in order to have freedom and greater quality of life. In 1991, he gave up his professional life, dedicating himself exclusively to his company. Since then, he has trained thousands of people and presented Entrepreneurship and Leadership conferences to more than 400,000 people around the world. Today, his company is present in more than 20 countries.